Rose Coppin

& now for
with love,
2/8 ₤2.00 Mother.

GW00982756

THE CINQUE PORTS
AND ROMNEY MARSH

The Cinque Ports and Romney Marsh

MARGARET BRENTNALL

JOHN GIFFORD LTD.
LONDON

First published in Great Britain
1972 by John Gifford Ltd,
125 Charing Cross Road,
London WC2H oEB

SBN 70710223 5

Printed in Great Britain by
Cox & Wyman Ltd,
London, Fakenham and Reading

Contents

List of Illustrations

All photographs are by the author unless otherwise indicated beneath the illustration concerned.

Acknowledgments

In writing this book I have been greatly aided by many people, and although I cannot list them all I wish to mention those to whom I am especially indebted.

Mr. W. H. Dyer of Hastings has provided me with a wealth of information on the Cinque Port where he has spent his life— it was he, in fact, who first opened my eyes many years ago to the infinite charm of the Old Town of Hastings. I also owe thanks to the following: to Mr. and Mrs. J. B. L. Clark of Winchelsea for much help on detail in connection with their Ancient Town, including the use by Mr. Clark of his Jurat's key for the Winchelsea Museum during its period of winter closure. To Mr. and Mrs. Harry Margary of Lympne Castle for sharing with me their researches on the historic castle which is their home. To Mr. Claude Paine of Lydd for regaling me with stories of the Romney Marsh countryside and for information on the famous breed of sheep which his family has reared in the Marsh for generations. To Mr. Bob Scott, Warden of the Royal Society for the Protection of Birds' reserve at Dungeness for advice on the bird population of the Marshland area and the changes brought about as agriculture, in some areas, usurps the pastureland and the true watery habitat. To Mr. and Mrs. Duthoit of the Manor Farm, Court-at-Street, for allowing me to approach the ruined chapel of the Holy Maid of Kent by way of their land. To Mr. Gordon Busby, Town Sergeant of Sandwich for describing so fully the background and traditions of this once great, and now inland, Cinque Port. To Mr. Reginald Leppard, former Town Sergeant of Dover, who gave me much information and entrusted to my care his valuable and long out-of-print books on the history of Dover; and to Mr. W. Errington, the present Town Sergeant, for his willing help during my visit to Dover. To Mr. Geoffrey Bagley and his team of helpers at the Rye Museum; and to Mr. George Fearon, also of Rye, for delving into the baptismal records of

St. Mary's Church on my behalf. To the Rectors and Vicars who were so ready to help with permission to photograph and with information on their churches – and in this respect to Miss Anne Roper for the vastly informative guides which she has provided for a number of the Marshland churches. To the County Archivists of Lewes and Maidstone, and especially to Dr. Felix Hull, Kent County Archivist, for his prompt replies when bombarded with eleventh-hour queries. To Mr. J. R. Sperr, antiquarian and second-hand bookseller of Highgate Village, London, who was indefatigable in obtaining out-of-print and reputedly unobtainable reference books. To Mr. Cyril Palmer for reading the proofs and making some most valuable suggestions and corrections. And finally to my sister, not only for careful reading of both typescript and proofs, but also for accompanying me on my exploration of the Cinque Ports and Marsh with as much enthusiasm as I felt myself.

Highgate, London   MARGARET BRENTNALL

1. Historic Background of Cinque Ports and Marsh

There is no more historic area in Britain than the south-east coast of England—the Cinque Ports coastline of Kent and Sussex and the marshland country which lies between Hythe and Rye. This was the 'invasion shore' where the Romans, Saxons, Danes and Normans landed, and where other would-be invaders had also hoped to land. At Sandwich are the remains of the vast Roman fortress of Richborough—the Rutupiae of the Romans; at Dover the Pharos still survives whose light guided the Roman ships into harbour; at Hastings are the remains of the Norman castle built in the days of the Conqueror; and along the Cinque Ports shore—at Deal, Walmer and Camber—are the still-intact castles built by Henry VIII to fend off the invasion-crusade preached by the Pope, which never materialized; between Hythe and Rye flows the Royal Military Canal constructed to repel Napoleon's army, as were the Martello Towers which are still to be seen, like outsize pepper-pots, along this coast.

The Five Ports are, in fact, seven, and their correct title is the Cinque Ports and Two Ancient Towns. They comprise Hastings, Romney, Hythe, Dover, Sandwich, Winchelsea and Rye, and attached to them throughout the centuries have been a varying number of member towns. In medieval times the Cinque Ports represented a maritime confederation of massive importance, on which fell reponsibility for the naval defence of this vulnerable coast and of the Channel crossing. Today most of them are no longer ports at all; the sea and the shifting coastline conquered where no other enemy could. Only Dover of the seven, retains its status as a great port.

In the past centuries the people of the Ports and the Marsh had two characteristics in common—their spirit of independence and lawlessness. These led, at different periods, to the Portsmen's taste for piracy and the Marshmen's enthusiasm for smuggling. But however unruly they were, their services

B

in ensuring the safety of the Channel and of the Marsh were so important to the monarch that their failings were overlooked. Thus they enjoyed liberties in excess of other parts of the country. These liberties constituted, in fact, a form of self-government, and they fostered the people's natural independence and high-handedness.

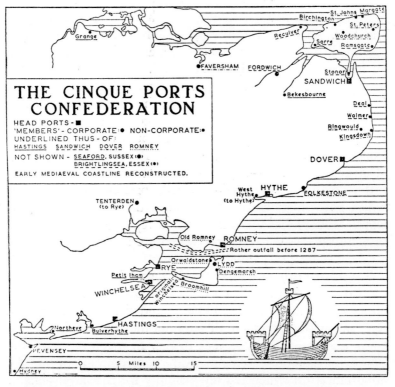

1. The Cinque Ports Confederation, with early medieval coastline reconstructed. *Reproduced from 'Kent History Illustrated' by permission of the Kent Education Committee and R. R. Sellman.*

To take one example of Marsh lawlessness—for a town to receive royal permission to hold a market and a fair was a favour much sought after in medieval times; but Lydd and Brookland, in the Marsh, both went ahead and held their markets and fairs without any right to do so at all. No word of their activities would reach higher levels, they thought, and certainly the secretive Marshland people would breathe no word to a stranger. But they did not get away with this indefinitely, and retribution followed.

The self-governing body of this remote area was entitled the Lords of the Level of Romney Marsh, and it consisted of a Bailiff and 23 Jurats with power to levy their own taxes for upkeep of the sea walls and watercourses and also to seize sand and soil from landowners' property for the walls' repair. This governing body became the two Corporations—the Lords, Bailiff and Jurats of Romney Marsh, and the Bailiff, Jurats and Commonalty of Romney Marsh. Their ancient Courts and the jurisdiction they administered are of outstanding interest, for the Charter of Romney Marsh comprised the first code of land drainage law in this country. The word 'Level' refers to a self-contained land drainage district, and 'Liberty' to the area whose privilege of self-government, granted by the Crown, made it independent of the King's Sheriff or officers. Only as late as 1950 did an Act of Parliament bring to an end the jurisdiction of the Lords of the Level, with all the fascinating traditions involved. Why? There is enthusiasm enough for trying to revive old customs which have died a natural death, yet here was something of great antiquity which had survived since 'time out of mind' as the old charters would say.

These Courts and the Charter of Romney Marsh represent the law-abiding side of the Marsh of the old days. Where drainage and sea-wall protection were concerned the Marshmen were prepared to conform. On the other side of the picture, they were an isolated and secretive community where smuggling was rife, and even the churches were used as 'hides' for contraband. The Marshmen were not averse to a bit of wrecking, and if a vessel with a rich cargo could be lured ashore by false fires this was deemed a good night's work. Even today there is an uncommunicative streak in the true families of the Marsh, a heritage of the distant days of the smugglers and wreckers.

Most people who come to Romney Marsh for the first time either dislike it instantly or are fascinated. One thing is certain, it is a place apart, with its own strange character and

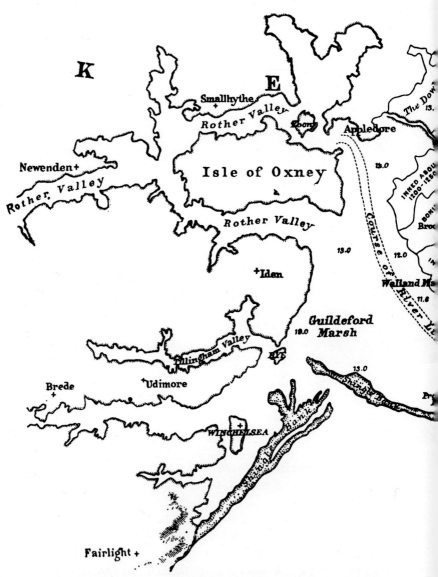

K

E

Smallhythe

Rother Valley

Boong

Appledore

The Dow

13.

13.0

INNED ABOU
1200-1250

Newenden+

Rother Valley

Isle of Oxney

Bong

Broo

Rother Valley

19.0

Course of River

Walland Ma

12.0

11.5

+Iden

Guildeford
Marsh

19.0

Tillingham Valley

Brede
+

+Udimore

13.0

WINCHELSEA

Pr

Fairlight +

2. Map of medieval Romney, Walland, Denge and Guildeford Marshes
(from Lewin's *Invasion of Britain by Julius Caesar,* 1862).
"Guildeford Marsh" is now known as Guldeford Level.

Aldington

Lymne

Hythe

ehorne

10.6

9.6

8.6

8.0

T

11.6

8.6   8.8   8.8

8.0

N   ROMNEY MARSH

10.0

11.6

All Romney Marsh Proper was reclaimed at once
by the erection of Rhee Wall from Appledore to
Romney, but by whom the work was executed is
uncertain.   Some refer it to the Bilge of
ancient Britain who brought the art of em-
banking from the Netherlands, others give the
credit to the Romans. The Marsh was certain-
8.6 ly under cultivation in the time of the
Romans, as Roman remains are found
extensively over the
whole area.

7.0

7.0

6.0

6.0

9.0

7.0

9.6   5.0   5.0

4.0

Old
Romney

ROMNEY

MAP OF
ROMNEY, WALLAND, DENGE
AND GUILDEFORD MARSHES.
shewing
what Lands had been Inned previous
to the 14th Century.

The figures denote the depth (in feet) of
the present surface below High Water Mark
(Medium Spring Tides)

N.B. The Innings beyond the limits of
the Marshes are not noticed.

(From Lewin's Invasion of Britain
by Julius Cæsar, 1862.)

Midley

Lydd

Denge Marsh

Shingle Bank

DENGENESS

Scale of Miles

1 ½ 0 1 2 3 4 5 6.

history; its great lonely churches, twisting lanes and dykes, its mists, and the flocks of Romney Marsh sheep are an intrinsic part of the scene. The Reverend Richard H. Barham, author of *The Ingoldsby Legends* and incumbent for a while at Snargate, was quoting a local saying when he wrote 'The world, according to the best geographers, is divided into Europe, Asia, Africa, America and Romney Marsh.'

Long ago most of this land was covered by the sea. Below the inland cliff at Lympne the great Roman harbour of Portus Lemanis once lay, and to the Romans is generally attributed the construction of the Rhee Wall which stretched from Romney to Appledore and was the first step in reclaiming the land which has become Romney Marsh. Some authorities believe that the Rhee Wall was built earlier, by the British Belgae people who were conquered by the Romans, and there is also the point of view which doubts whether it ever was a sea wall, believing that it was purely an embanked watercourse running from Snargate to the sea.

But it is dangerous to get involved in these controversies over the Rhee Wall, the evolution of the Marsh, the eastward drift, and the tides and wave action which have caused the build-up of shingle banks and are still adding to the shingle territory of Dungeness. Readers who wish to study this very specialized angle of the Marsh and Cinque Ports coastline will find an authoritative source in the bibliography.

The later drainage of Romney Marsh's neighbour Walland Marsh, between the twelfth and sixteenth centuries, reflects its monastic ownership in the names of the 'innings' (the term by which the drainage operations are known) – for instance, the Boniface, Baldwin's and St. Thomas's innings. Today drainage of the whole area is so efficient that true marshland no longer exists; instead there is pasturage together with areas of cultivated land of outstanding fertility.

The land which lies, with its patchwork of dykes, below the inland cliff at Lympne is the true Romney Marsh. The whole area between Hythe and Rye tends to bear this name, whereas it is, in fact, composed of Romney, Walland and Denge Marshes in Kent, and the Guldeford Level in Sussex (from the county boundary to Rye). The territory of Romney

Marsh itself stretches from Hythe westwards to New Romney, then north along the line of the Rhee Wall to Appledore, after which the boundary follows 'the cliff' and the Military Canal back to Hythe. The whole area known by the composite term of the Marsh covers about 50,000 acres, and on its fringe are four of the Cinque Port Towns—Hythe, New Romney, Winchelsea and Rye.

The history of the Cinque Ports dates back to the eleventh century and the reign of Edward the Confessor. In the early days the Head Ports were Hastings, Romney, Hythe, Dover and Sandwich, while Winchelsea and Rye qualified only as Members of Hastings. In the course of time these two 'Ancient Towns' were raised to independent Head Port status, with comparable services and privileges. In addition, over 30 other towns and fishing villages were recognized at various times either as Corporate Members (confirmed by Charter) or Non-corporate Members (having only an informal link with their parent Port). It was not until after the Norman Conquest that the Cinque Ports were fortified, and only during the reign of Edward I that the Confederation *as a whole* had its services and privileges established in legal form by the Royal Charter of 1278.

The services consisted of supplying ships and seamen for the King's use for defence of the coast and the sea passage, which meant, in medieval times, providing the nucleus of the royal fleet. The power of the Cinque Ports was, therefore, immense. In consequence their privileges were unique. These are, however, expressed in Edward I's Charter of 1278 in words so unintelligible today that one is left little the wiser unless, as in the Hythe Museum, a glossary is attached.

The King decreed that, among other privileges, the Cinque Ports should be quit of Lastage (duty by weight), Tallage (duty by number), Passage (tax on landing), Rivage (wharf toll), Ponsage (bridge toll), Infangtheff (the right to judge thieves taken within their precincts), Utfangtheff (the right to judge thieves from the Ports). He granted the much-valued Honours at Court, and also the right of wreck, the latter an important privilege, for in territories which lay outside the liberties of the Cinque Ports the King claimed whatever was washed ashore without any living creature upon it. He also granted Den and Strond at Yarmouth in Norfolk.

It was Den and Strond that caused most of the trouble. This gave the Cinque Portsmen the right to land, without fee, at Yarmouth, to sell their fish and dry their nets on the strand— and they were also placed in control of the annual Yarmouth Herring Fair. It seems that the Cinque Portsmen had sent Bailiffs to Yarmouth and taken over control of the annual Herring Fair before their rights in this respect had ever been regulated by charter. So dominant was their sense of rightful control that when the Bishop of Norwich established a priest at Yarmouth to pray for the success of the herring catch, the Portsmen dismissed him and provided a priest of their own choosing. King John tended to take the side of the Norfolk fishermen and, in granting them privileges, upset the truculent Portsmen, so that intolerance and enmity flourished. Almost undeclared war between the Portsmen and the Norfolk fishermen was the result. They loathed each other most heartily, and many deaths resulted from skirmishes on the Yarmouth shore. On one occasion a Bailiff of the Cinque Ports was killed by a Yarmouth Bailiff, for which deed the survivor received short shrift and was duly hanged.

One instance of the animosity which existed between the Portsmen and the men of Yarmouth appears in the Chronicle of Matthew Paris, the monk of St. Albans who recorded so vividly the events of the reign of Henry III. In the year 1254 he writes that, 'As the queen was now preparing to set sail for the continent, the inhabitants of Yarmouth sent a large and handsome ship, manned with thirty skilful sailors, and well armed, to be at the service of the Prince Edward, to convey him and his attendants across the channel in greater security. The people of Winchelsea had prepared some ships for the conveyance of the queen, and finding that the one sent for the prince was much larger and more handsome than theirs, they grew jealous, and treacherously and suddenly made an attack on it, destroying the ship, and wounding and slaying some of the crew; and in order to palliate their crime, they took the mast of the destroyed vessel, and fitted it to the queen's ship as though they had acted as they did for her benefit and advantage. The Yarmouth people thereupon made heavy complaints of this proceeding, not only to the queen and to Earl Richard, but also to all the wardens of the Cinque Ports and with justice roused the whole kingdom to take vengeance for the offence.'

But the worst outbreak between the two factions was in 1297 when Edward I's navy was gathering to oppose the French fleet. A fine and mighty contingent of ships was assembling—until the Cinque Portsmen sighted the Yarmouth ships. They forgot the common enemy, and in the battle which resulted 32 of the Yarmouth ships were destroyed and 200 Yarmouth men killed. It can be imagined what Edward I's sentiments were. He commanded that in future the Cinque Ports and Yarmouth ships were to be kept at a distance!

Between 1287 and 1306 there were so many fights on the Yarmouth shore that the King had to intervene on the side of the Norfolk fishermen. But the seafaring Portsmen, with buccaneering and piracy in their blood, were difficult to restrain. They were well aware that for defence of the coast and the Channel crossing their services were vital—for the loss of Normandy during the reign of King John had transformed the peaceful Channel into a dangerously narrow sea barrier between hostile countries. In dealing with king and people they knew that they held the trump card—even to the extent, on occasion, of flouting the King's will.

Only in the reign of Henry VIII did the Cinque Ports cease sending Bailiffs to Yarmouth and the long feud came to an end.

The men of the Cinque Ports were sworn to keep watch and ward, but this did not include land service. In the seventeenth century Charles I called upon the Cinque Ports to raise 300 men for land service—a call which the Portsmen firmly ignored. The Constable of Dover Castle was then ordered to levy a tax of £3 per man up to £900—which all the Cinque Ports, with the exception of Rye, continued to ignore. This was not the last time that the Cinque Ports were asked to supply men for land service, the very service from which they considered themselves exempt.

The Customals (Rolls of the Laws and Customs) of the

Cinque Ports and Two Ancient Towns were all originally deposited at Dover Castle, having been compiled in the fourteenth century (though dating back in usage to much earlier times) on the order of Roger Mortimer, Earl of March, Lord Warden of the Cinque Ports and Constable of Dover Castle. The penalties for lawbreakers contained in these Customals make intriguing reading today. In the Dover Customal, for instance, is a penalty which one cannot help thinking would soon put an end to pickpockets and shop-lifters today. It reads as follows: '. . . if there be a cutpurse or a private picker, that be taken with the money within the Franchise, anon he shall be led before the Mayor, Bailiff and Jurats, and if he may not excuse himself reasonably of the misdeed, though there be no suit against him, the Mayor and Bailiff shall set him before the Sergeant on the pillory, and all the people that will come there may do him villany, and after that they may cut off his ear and lead him to the furthest part of the Franchise and then he shall forswear the Town and the said Franchise and if he come again at any time they may by the same usage cut off the other ear.'

There was a bit of trouble in Dover on one occasion when a pickpocket, who had been nailed to the pillory by his ear, was handed a knife to cut his ear off and set himself free; this, however, was strictly outside the rules, and there had to be a 'Hornblowing' (as the Common Assemblies were called) to look into so serious an irregularity. His ear should have been sliced off by the Bailiff!

This ear-cutting penalty could cause misunderstandings for anyone who lost an ear by honest means. A letter exists which was written by King John to Robert FitzRobert in 1203 and is of interest in this connection. It reads: 'The King, to all to whom these presents shall come: Greeting. Know ye that Robert, the son of Robert the mercer, lost his ear at Chateau-neuf-sur-Sart in our service and not on account of felony. And this we certify to you, that you may know it. Witness ourself, at Montfort, the 23rd day of July.'

Punishments were grim in medieval times, and if the crime merited more than ear-cutting a thief at Dover was led to the top of a hill called Sharpness from which he was cast down.

At Winchelsea he was hanged in the Salt Marsh. At Sandwich he was buried alive in Gallows Field. Anyone tried by the Court of Shepway and condemned to death was placed immediately on a sledge and drawn round the circuit of Shepway, then hanged there.

It was a ruthless age. Many times in this book the ferocity of the French raiders of the Cinque Ports is recorded, but it must be remembered that the Cinque Portsmen themselves did not hang back in this respect. The French soldiers were retaliating as often as not, and in 1242 the Cinque Ports were granted leave to ravage the French coast, with a fifth of the spoil to go to the King; the only restriction was that the churches should be spared. The Ports indulged themselves with a will—according to Matthew Paris 'cruelly exceeding the limit prescribed by the King and robbing and killing English as well as French'.

Only after the civil war of the thirteenth century, when the Portsmen sided with Simon de Montfort against Henry III, did the King take steps to bring the Ports under closer sovereign control with the creation of the office of Lord Warden of the Cinque Ports—a royal appointment united with that of Constable of Dover Castle (although some form of Wardenship had existed long previously). Before taking up his duties every new Lord Warden gave his pledge before a gathering of the Ports' representatives that he would uphold their liberties.

The courts of Shepway, Brodhull and Guestling were created to handle the joint affairs of the Cinque Ports, and much the earliest was the Court of Shepway. This is known to have existed by the middle of the twelfth century, when the Barons of the Cinque Ports could claim trial in this Court. But with the royal appointment of a Lord Warden, who presided over the 'Kynges high courte of Shepway', it became a means by which the monarch could control the Ports and Portsmen (to some extent at least) when they were at the height of their power. The Court of Brodhull and the Court of Guestling (which finally combined as the Brotherhood and Guestling) were established by the Portsmen themselves to protect the privileges of the Cinque Ports. Today the main reason for a meeting of the Court of Shepway is the installation of a new Lord Warden, and as this is a life appointment the meetings are rare.

Henry VIII issued an order governing the uniform to be worn by the Cinque Portsmen, and this reads: '. . . everie person who goeth into the navy of the Portis shal have a cote of white cotyn with a red crosse and the arms of the Portis underneath; that is to say the halfe lyon and the halfe ship.'

In early times Freemen of the Ports all bore the title of 'Baron of the Cinque Ports'. Gradually this honour became much less general, and today it is only allotted to the Freemen elected to attend a coronation. (It has no connection with the great feudal barons of medieval times.)

Honours at court constituted one of the most highly cherished privileges granted to the Cinque Ports, and included the task of bearing the canopy which used to be held above the monarch's head as he walked in procession at his coronation. The occasion of Henry III and Queen Eleanor's coronation in 1236 is described by Matthew Paris, who records that 'the Barons of the Cinque Ports carried over the King wherever he went the silken cloth four-square, purple, supported by four silvered spears with four little silver-gilt bells, four Barons being assigned to every spear, according to the diversity of the Ports, lest Port should seem to be preferred to Port. Likewise the same bore a silken cloth over the Queen coming after the King, which said cloths they claim as theirs of right, and they obtained them at Court.'

Not only the canopy itself, but the decorative bells and the silver staves became, at each coronation, the trophy of the Barons, to be shared between the Cinque Ports. Samuel Pepys has left us an account of the coronation of Charles II in 1661, and in describing the scene afterwards at Westminster Hall he writes: 'And the King came in with his crowne on, his sceptre in his hand, under a canopy borne up by silver staves, carried by Barons of the Cinque Ports, and little bells at every end . . .'

But all was not well for the Barons on this occasion. On arriving at the foot of the stairway inside Westminster Hall they turned decorously to take their allotted place of honour at the first banqueting table at the right hand of the King – whereupon the King's footmen attempted to seize their trophy. The Barons swiftly clutched it, the footmen clutched it, and the canopy, Barons and footmen were dragged the length of the hall in a scuffle for possession. Only after the intervention of York Herald and the King's command for arrest of the footmen did the Barons return victorious to the banquet. But alas, their place of honour had been usurped, and they were forced to swallow their pride as well as their dinner at the bottom of the second table.

At the next coronation, in 1685, Pepys himself was among the Barons who supported the canopy of James II. But by that time he had closed the pages of his diary, otherwise we might have had one of the pithiest descriptions ever recorded of the coronation duties of a Baron of the Cinque Ports.

The coronation of George IV in 1821 witnessed another scuffle between the Barons and those who would rob them of their trophy. Once again they emerged victorious, but this was to prove the last occasion on which the canopy was used. The right of the Barons of the Cinque Ports to have an honoured place at coronations was somewhat cursorily ignored by William IV and Queen Victoria, but at Edward VII's coronation, and subsequently, places of honour have been reserved for them in Westminster Abbey.

The office of Lord Warden survives today but its character has changed. Formerly one of the most powerful appointments in the realm, it is now a prestige rather than an active post—an honour granted at the end of a great career of loyalty and service. Just how great an honour it is can be judged by the names of some of the Lords Warden of the nineteenth and twentieth centuries—William Pitt, the Duke of Wellington, Sir Winston Churchill, and the present Lord Warden, Sir Robert Menzies.

It was not only the shifting coastline and loss of harbours that caused the final decline of the Ports—their unique power was at an end when a Royal Navy came into being. Its creation began with the Tudors, and the man who played a major part in the Royal Navy's seventeenth-century development was a Baron of the Cinque Ports himself, Samuel Pepys, the

1. **Barons of the Cinque Ports** bearing the royal canopy at the coronation of King James II in 1685. The diarist Samuel Pepys, as Secretary of the Admiralty and a Coronation Baron, is seen bearing the front left-hand stave.

A. The *KINGS* Majestie.
B. The Bishop of Durham.
C. The Bishop of Bath and Wells.
D. Four Earls Eldest Sons.
E. The Master of the Robes.

F. Sixteen Barons of the Cinqueports.
G. The Earl of Huntingdon Capt. of the Band of G.ᵉ Pensioners.
H. The Duke of Northumberland Capt of the Guard in Waiting.
I. The Vicount Grandison Capt of the yeomen of the Guard.
K. Gentlemen Pensioners.

diarist. But during subsequent years, and during the two world wars of this century, the men of the Ports proved themselves as valiant as ever.

The list of the Head Ports and their member towns varies throughout the centuries, but Charles ɪɪ's Charter of 1668 is the one usually quoted and this is given below:

Head Port.	Corporate Members.	Non-corporate Members.
Hastings	Pevensey, Seaford	Bulverhythe, Petit Iham, Hidney, Beakesbourne, Grange, alias Grenche.
New Romney	Lydd	Broomhill, Old Romney, Dengemarsh, Oswardstone.
Hythe	—	West Hythe.
Dover	Folkestone, Faversham	Margate, St. John's, Goresend, Birchington Wood alias Woodchurch, St. Peter's, Kingsdown, Ringwould.
Sandwich	Fordwich	Deal, Walmer, Ramsgate, Stonar, Sarre, Brightlingsea.
Rye	Tenterden	—
Winchelsea	—	—

Deal eventually far outstripped Fordwich in status and maritime importance, despite being only a Non-corporate Member at the time of this Charter. Deal, Margate and Ramsgate are all now Corporate Members; Pevensey, Seaford and Fordwich have become Non-corporate.

In the following chapters I am going to lead the way through the Romney Marsh countryside and to each of the historic Head Ports in turn, tracing their past and discovering them as they are today. I shall not make a direct tour from west to east, as the Cinque Ports listing indicates, but will set out

from Hythe, for here the superb view of the Marsh, from the
Shepway Cross and from the escarpment at Lympne, provides
an ideal introduction to the whole area. The route will con-

Ray Warner, Dover.

2. The Banner of the Cinque Ports, which was used in past days at the
opening of the Yarmouth Herring Fair. The Cinque Portsmen were granted
control of this important Fair, with right to land, sell their fish and dry their
nets on the Yarmouth strand. The banner is preserved in the Council Chamber
of the Maison Dieu at Dover.

tinue along the crest of the inland cliff which has been left
high and dry by the seas, and then to each of the Cinque Port
towns whose ships and men were, for centuries, the guardians
and defenders of the 'invasion shore'.

2. Hythe

Hythe is ideally placed for anyone who wishes to explore all the Cinque Ports, the clifftop road, and Romney Marsh. Like so many of the Confederation's historic towns today, it is a Cinque Port without a port, and it is so long since its harbour existed that the days of ships are forgotten. Fishing boats still sail from the beach half a mile away, but the town has a different character from that of a port and the seafaring activity it brings; and given the choice its citizens would probably not wish it otherwise. It is an attractive small town, with historic associations in abundance, two great castles (Saltwood and Lympne) on its outskirts, and the Royal Military Canal flowing through its midst as a reminder of the days of the Napoleonic threat.

The town's status as one of the Confederation's Head Ports is, however, far from forgotten, and the Shepway Cross on a grassy mound beside the Hythe to Lympne road marks the traditional meeting-place in early times of the ancient Court of Shepway over which the Lord Warden of the Cinque Ports presided. Among the Cinque Ports records held at Dover is a report of the proceedings of the Court of Shepway which took place at 'the Shepway crossroads' on 14 April 1358, at which the Lord Warden was Roger Mortimer, Earl of March, and 65 Barons of the Cinque Ports attended.

Hythe was an important place as far back as pre-Conquest days, and its natural harbour was formed by the creek which cut inland to West Hythe. As the centuries rolled by, however, the inland extremity of the creek silted up, shingle accumulated along the foreshore, and the sea receded. Thus Hythe's seaside resort is today on land formerly covered by the waves, while the old town clings to the hillside half a mile inland. The creek has disappeared altogether.

It was in the eleventh century, during the reign of King Canute, that the Manor of Saltwood, of which Hythe formed

3. **St. Leonard's Church,** Hythe. The remarkable height of the chancel (higher than the nave) can be seen in this picture. The thirteenth-century D-shaped tower contains the stairway leading to the triforium and clerestory.

part, was granted to the Priory of Christchurch in Canterbury; and after the Conquest, when a division of monastic lands took place, this Manor passed to the first Norman Archbishop of Canterbury, Archbishop Lanfranc. It remained the property of his successors until, during Henry VIII's reign, Hythe and Saltwood became the property of the Crown. Thereafter Hythe's senior official was a Bailiff appointed by the Crown, and only in 1575, under Queen Elizabeth I's Royal Charter, did the town gain control of its affairs, with the right to choose its own Mayor, to possess lands, and to hold a fair.

The last Bailiff and the first Mayor was, in fact, one and the same man, John Bredgman—so in this case the Crown's choice had obviously been a popular one. Among the treasures of the Parish Church of St. Leonard is the monumental brass of 1581 which commemorates John Bredgman, last Bailiff and first Mayor. The inscription reads:

> While he did live whiche heare doth lie,
> Three Sutes gatt he of ye Crowne,
> The Mortmaine, fayer and Mayraltie,
> For Hythe, this antient Towne.
> And was him self the Baylye last,
> And Mayer fyrste by name,
> Thoughe he bee gone tyme is not paste
> To Preayse God for ye same.

In medieval times Hythe does not seem to have suffered the series of sackings and burnings by the French which figure so drastically in the annals of some of the other Ports. According to Hasted's account, an ominously large French fleet approached Hythe in 1293 and succeeded in landing up to 200 men in the haven, but 'the townsmen came upon them and slew every one of them; upon which the rest of the fleet hoisted sail, and made no further attempt'.

This was a splendid display of spirit and defiance, but if the French did less harm to Hythe than they did to Rye and Winchelsea, the sea and the shingle were foes over which no such victory could be claimed. A succession of other disasters also afflicted the Port. In 1348 the dreaded Black Death attacked the townspeople, striking with merciless indifference the young and able-bodied as well as the old, and leaving terrible gaps in the roll of citizens. Then, in 1400, when the Black Death had become a nightmare memory, the Plague took a further drastic toll of the community. This was not all, for fire broke out among the closely-built timber and thatch houses, rapidly becoming so violent a conflagration that hundreds of homes were destroyed. A final blow was the loss of up to five Hythe ships and about 100 men in a terrible storm at sea.

In a superstitious age such a series of disasters could mean only one thing—that the Port was accursed and that the people, like their fellow Portsmen of long ago at Old Winchelsea, should leave and build a new town and port on less fateful ground. They were dissuaded from this by a project to build a new harbour, and Henry IV, as some form of compensation for all their trials, released Hythe from ship service until the Port should have recovered from its series of disasters.

In the fifteenth century great efforts were made to ease the silting-up process which was destroying the harbour. In fact, a new harbour was constructed, and according to the Hythe Records its completion was celebrated with great festivity and high hopes; but the sea and the silt and the shingle won the day in the end. No trace of this harbour survives.

Today the life of the community is divided between the resort, on the sea-front, and the old town half a mile inland, on the hillside. The latter has some enchanting old houses hidden away in its narrow roads and steep alleyways. Predominant among them, facing the incline to the church, is the Old Manor House, whose earliest parts date from the mid-seventeenth century. This was the home of the Deedes family, who rebuilt the south transept of the church in 1750, incorporating the Deedes Chapel and burial vault. Their coat of arms, displayed in the church, takes for its motto *Facta non Verba*, meaning Deeds not Words. The family eventually moved into the countryside north of the town, where they built the mansion of Sandling Park whose gardens are noted today for their rhododendron displays in spring. Members of the Deedes family also owned Saltwood Castle for well over 100 years, from the end of the eighteenth century.

A short but steep road climbs from the Old Manor House to St. Leonard's Church. Built in 1100, St. Leonard's first consisted solely of nave and a small chancel which ended where the present lofty chancel begins. In 1165 the church was enlarged and then, in 1220, the chancel was built which is one of St. Leonard's most remarkable features. It is outstanding in many respects: in being so lofty that it is higher than the nave itself; in having both triforium and clerestory; and in the dignity of its approach by a flight of nine steps. The vaulted roof gives an impression of restoration, and this was, in fact, constructed in 1887 to the original thirteenth-century designs. When the chancel was first built preliminary construction of this vaulted roof was started, but something—no one seems quite clear what it was—caused the work to be suspended.

The church's thirteenth-century tower collapsed in 1739, when an earth tremor caused the upper half to come tumbling down. Earth tremors provide no warning, and it happened that about ten people were waiting in the porch at the time, about to climb the tower for the view from the top. They missed the view but kept their lives—all because of delay in fetching the key! Six years went by before a start was made on rebuilding the tower, and it was then discovered to be perilously ruinous. Demolition followed and complete rebuilding began in 1750, so the stately tower of this ancient building dates only from the eighteenth century.

One of the treasures of St. Leonard's Church which greatly intrigues visitors today is the marvellous iron chest of about the year 1500 in which are stored the church registers. The main lock is linked with a series of eleven bolts, all so heavy that a lever is needed to turn the key.

Even more intriguing to visitors with a taste for the macabre is the collection of skulls and thigh bones in the thirteenth-century crypt. This vaulted passageway was never, in fact, a crypt at all, but was constructed as an ambulatory when the closeness of the road made it impossible for the processional path to encircle the church without leaving consecrated ground. At some time or other—possibly when the Plague caused so many deaths that space had to be made in the burial ground—these bones were placed here; and here they remained, skull upon skull, thigh bone upon thigh bone. There are said to be about 8,000 thigh bones and possibly 1,500 skulls, and their date has been attributed to between A.D. 1200 and 1400.

The skulls differ from British types, and it has been suggested that they represent the descendants of the Romans, or people who settled here from Europe during the Occupation

Jack C. Adams, Hythe.

4. Skulls and thigh bones, stacked in vast numbers in the crypt of St. Leonard's Church at Hythe.

and stayed when the Romans departed. In most instances death was natural, for there are few signs of wounds or violence; the teeth are good, but many of the bones show evidence of rheumatism, the gift of the neighbouring marshland damp.

George Borrow visited the crypt as a child of just under four years of age, in the company of his mother and small brother, and in *Lavengro* (published in 1851) he describes the effect which the crypt had upon him:

'"Skulls, Madam," said the sexton; "skulls of the old Danes! Long ago they came pirating into these parts; and then there chanced a mighty shipwreck for God was angry with them, and He sunk them; these skulls as they came ashore were placed here as a memorial. There were many more when I was young, but now they are fast disappearing. Some of them must have belonged to strange fellows, Madam. Only see that one; why the two young gentry can scarcely lift it." And indeed, my brother and myself had entered Golgotha, and commenced handling these gloomy relics of mortality. One enormous skull, lying in a corner, had fixed our attention, and we had drawn it forth. Spirit of eld, what a skull was yon! I never forgot the Daneman's skull . . . and if, long after, when I became a student, I devoted myself with peculiar zest to Danish lore and the acquirement of the old Norse tongue and its dialects, I can only explain this by the early impression received at Hythe from the tale of the old sexton and the sight of the Danish skull.'

The sexton did not prove accurate in his statement, but he made a good tale of it, as sextons sometimes do, and its influence was long-lasting on this small and imaginative boy. But surely George Borrow, not yet four years of age, had a remarkable memory for dialogue! The 'Daneman's skull' is now represented in St. Leonard's crypt only by a plaster cast, for the original is in the possession of the Royal College of Surgeons.

In St. Leonard's churchyard is the grave of Lionel Lukin (1742–1834), whose invention of the life-boat was patented in 1785. Twenty years earlier a Frenchman named de Bernières had produced an unsinkable boat, but this does not seem to have been put to practical use; therefore the honour goes to an Englishman of having produced the first means by which countless men, women and children have escaped death at sea.

In South Shields, County Durham, William Wouldhave was

5. **Grave of Lionel Lukin,** life-boat inventor, at Hythe.

at about the same time experimenting along similar lines—and
on his grave, too, the claim is made that *he* invented the life-
boat. Wouldhave's special contribution was in producing the
model of an unsinkable self-righting life-boat. Working on his
model, Henry Greathead (also of South Shields) built the
first boat designed from the outset as a life-boat and used for
that purpose. Lukin's first life-boat was a conversion from a
fishing-boat. In the early days of life-boats both the Lukin and
Greathead types were in use and achieved heroic rescues.

One fascinating aspect of Lukin's invention is the fact that this south-east corner of England, with its history of wreckers and smugglers, should have produced so humane an invention as the life-boat, and also some of the most gallant teams of life-boatmen on record. The story is told, however, that the man to whom Lukin entrusted the task of testing his first boat in rough seas could not resist the temptation to use so unsinkable a vessel for smuggling—with the result that this precious craft was seized and destroyed.

Hythe also claims as a citizen born and bred Francis Pettit-Smith, who invented Britain's version of the first successful marine screw-propeller. His design was patented in 1836. In 1839 he amended his patent, and in that year the *Archimedes* was used for experimental purposes, driven by the Pettit-Smith screw-propeller. In 1843 H.M.S. *Rattler*, the first ship in the Royal Navy to be screw-propelled, adopted Pettit-Smith's design. His birth-place, Propeller House, is 31–33 in the High Street.

From unsinkable boats and marine screw-propellers it is a natural bit of chain-thinking to turn to today's form of locomotion, the motor car, and in St. Leonard's Church I came upon *A Motorist's Prayer*. The author and copyright are unknown, but the prayer is so apt, so beautifully worded, and so worth imprinting on the minds of all motorists, that I will repeat it here:

> Give me a steady hand, a watchful eye,
> That none may suffer hurt when I pass by.
> Thou givest life; I pray no act of mine
> May take away or mar that gift of Thine.
> Shield those, dear Lord, who bear me company,
> From foolish folk and all calamity.
> Teach me to use my car for others' need,
> Let me not miss, through witless love of speed,
> The beauties of thy world. That thus I may
> With joy and courtesy go on my way.

Yet another form of locomotion, which can truly be claimed to have gone on its way with joy and courtesy since the 1920's, is the narrow gauge (15-inch) Romney, Hythe and

Dymchurch Light Railway. The extent of the run is 14 miles, from Hythe to the Dungeness Lighthouse, and a trip on this railway is one of the delights of the summer season. The scale-model steam locomotives and coaches are just about as high as an average man's shoulder.

The Romney, Hythe and Dymchurch Light Railway was the creation of the well-known racing motorist, Captain J. E. P. Howey, whose enthusiasm for miniature railways took such practical form that it produced, in 1927, this intriguing little line, built with the blessing of the Southern Railway. It has never failed to give pleasure during peacetime, and during the years of the Second World War it proved to be anything but a plaything. One of its locomotives, armoured to meet the dangers of its new role, conveyed an anti-aircraft gun along this frontier shore, and also took part in the assembling of the Dungeness section of the 'Pluto' pipeline which kept a steady stream of petrol flowing beneath the Channel to the Allied invasion forces on the Continent. When Pluto was in full operation there were 17 of these under-ocean pipelines carrying petrol at the rate of a million gallons a day, and it is fascinating to know that this tiny railway shared, even on a miniature scale, in this vast operation.

No such role was contemplated when the building of Captain Howey's railway was embarked upon in 1925. Before it was completed, however, it had already achieved fame in having a royal driver, for in 1926 the future King George VI, then Duke of York, drove one of the trains along the first two completed miles of track. In 1927 came the ceremonial opening of the Hythe to New Romney stretch by the Lord Warden of the Cinque Ports, Lord Beauchamp; the extension to Dungeness followed two years later. The engines, nine in all, are scale replicas of famous main-line locomotives of former days, including five L.N.E.R. engines. Their names include *Winston Churchill* and *Doctor Syn*, and no names more appropriate to the area could have been found—the former commemorating one of the most famous of the Lords Warden of the Cinque Ports, and the latter representing the smuggler-parson who is possibly the best-known fictional character of the Romney Marsh coastline.

6. Church Hill, Hythe, is one of the most attractive of the streets which climb the hillside of the old town.

7. **Hythe's eighteenth-century Town Hall.** In the Council Chamber is a carved record of the Bailiffs from 1394 to 1574 and the Mayors from 1575 to the present date.

This little railway is not merely a fine-weather line. I once visited Dungeness in torrential rain when suddenly there was an imperious whistle, a collie dog rushed forward and stood with its front paws on top of a wire fence looking expectantly up the line—and then, through the downpour, came the tiny train; its engine was puffing forth steam valiantly, the passengers were sitting comfortably inside, and each coach looked as trim and neat as a new pin. The intrepid little train disappeared into the distance, towards Hythe.

The Museum at Hythe is small but of exceptional interest, for it provides an opportunity to study a full-size facsimile of the most important and historic of all the Cinque Ports Charters—Edward 1's Charter of 1278. The original is in the care of the Town Council, and is a treasured possession. Beside the Charter is an excellent glossary—invaluable in giving meaning to the unfamiliar words. Queen Elizabeth's Charter of 1575 is also displayed here—the one which enabled John Bredgman to be 'the Baylye last and Mayer fyrste'.

There are two features of present-day Hythe which linger especially in a visitor's mind—the Royal Military Canal and the sequence of Martello Towers along the Hythe shore. A special feature of the Canal is the Hythe Venetian Fête which takes place on alternate years, usually in August. I saw it years ago and have always remembered it, for what could be more pleasant on a fine summer's evening than to sit beside the Royal Military Canal and watch the elaborately-decorated boats and tableaux floating by.

But the Royal Military Canal and the Martello Towers are features of a much wider area than Hythe alone, and I shall make them the subject of my next chapter.

3. Napoleonic Defences—Military Canal and Martello Towers

The Royal Military Canal is the most peaceful of waterways. Trees cast their shadows upon its surface as it flows through Hythe, and sheep graze quietly beside it in the Romney Marsh countryside. Yet the Canal was never intended for peaceful use at all; it was built at the instigation of William Pitt (twice Premier, and Lord Warden of the Cinque Ports from 1792 until his death) as a defence measure against the threatened Napoleonic invasion.

The war with France lasted, in all, from 1793 to 1815, with a short and uneasy interval brought about by the Peace of Amiens (negotiated in 1801, but not signed until 1802). The Prime Minister at the time of the treaty was Addington, a leader who proved weak and unable to gain the confidence of the people. William Pitt had resigned the Premiership in 1801 over a conflict with George III on the question of Catholic rights in Ireland, but in May 1803 a state of war between England and France was again declared. Addington proved incapable of handling the crisis, and William Pitt was called upon, once more, to lead the country.

A popular couplet of the time runs, 'Pitt is to Addington, what London is to Paddington', and this sums up very well the general mood of relief that Pitt was again at the helm. During these years of danger Britain was blessed with three great leaders—Admiral Lord Nelson at sea, the Duke of Wellington on land, and William Pitt as Premier during the invasion threat.

When Pitt returned to power victory seemed remote and massive preparations for invasion were building up on the French coast. To Napoleon are attributed such statements as: 'With three days' east wind I could repeat the exploit of William the Conqueror', and 'Let us be masters of the Channel for six hours and we are masters of the world'.

While Napoleon gathered his fleet of flat-bottomed invasion

8. The Royal Military Canal in unmilitary mood as it flows through the centre of Hythe.

ships at Boulogne, armies of Volunteers were being enrolled along the English side of the Channel. Pitt became Colonel of the Cinque Ports Volunteers, and the camp-bed and folding chair which he used when out with them are still preserved at Walmer Castle. This was the time when the Royal Military Canal was being built, together with a string of Martello Towers along the shore.

These defences have been scoffed at as being too mild to stem any determined invasion force, but they were only part of a scheme of defence for which the preparatory time was

9. Martello Tower at Dymchurch. Several of these gaunt towers stand almost astride the Dymchurch Wall, the great barrier which, with its system of sluices, protects Romney Marsh from invasion by the sea.

short. The Royal Military Canal stretched from Hythe for 23 miles along the northern fringe of Romney Marsh to Appledore, then southwards to meet the river Rother at Rye. It was not a straight waterway as many people imagine but a defensive barrier with sharp bends or kinks at regular intervals, each kink planned as a cannon emplacement from which the invaders who attempted to cross the line of water which it commanded could be mown down. The Martello Towers provided gunfire on the shore, and there was a military road behind the Canal, concealed and protected by an earthwork, along which supplies and men could be moved rapidly. Additional plans included the removal of

c

10. A vista of **Martello Towers** along the sea shore at Hythe.

all animals that could provide food for the enemy, and a signalling system which would enable vital messages to reach
London in two minutes from the Downs (the naval anchorage in the channel between Deal and the Goodwin Sands).
Finally, the Marsh was to be flooded, and during a
meeting at Dymchurch between William Pitt and Generals
Moore and Twiss plans were made for the opening of the
sluices.

Patriotism and alarm mingled and ran high, but Pitt had the
complete confidence of town and countryfolk alike. He was a
rallying point of courage, just as Sir Winston Churchill was
during the Second World War. Rhymesters struck the mood
of the moment with verses that were patriotic but far from

immortal—such as the lines of John Wolcot (alias Peter Pindar, the pamphleteer and satirist) which ran:

> Come the Consul whenever he will,
> And he means to when Neptune is calmer.
> Pitt will send him a damned bitter pill
> From his fortress, the Castle of Walmer.

Then came the great naval Battle of Trafalgar on 21 October 1805, and the immediate threat of invasion was over. But Nelson was dead, killed in the hour of victory, and William Pitt was worn out by the strain; in January 1806 he died, at the early age of 46. The Duke of Wellington still had his mightiest victory ahead at Waterloo, and he alone of the famous trio survived to spend an old age of peace (and military orderliness) as Lord Warden of the Cinque Ports at Walmer Castle.

Thus the Royal Military Canal never saw any military action at all, and by 1806, the same year that its creator died, it was peacefully stocked with fish. For boating, fishing, or just sitting on its banks, it has been a delight ever since.

As the years passed the Canal scene became, in fact, so calm and unbelligerent that few could visualize its military capabilities at all, and the irrepressible Rev. Richard H. Barham, author of *The Ingoldsby Legends* (1840), pokes fun at it in *Mrs. Botherby's Story*. He writes: 'When the late Mr. Pitt was determined to keep out Buonaparte and prevent his gaining a settlement in the county of Kent, among other ingenious devices adopted for that purpose he caused to be constructed what was then, and has ever since been, conventionally termed a "Military Canal" . . . Trivial objections to the plan were made at the time by cavillers; and an old gentleman of the neighbourhood who proposed as a cheap substitute to put down his own cocked hat upon a pole, was deservedly pooh-pooh'd down; in fact, the job, though rather an expensive one, was found to answer remarkably well. The French managed, indeed, to scramble over the Rhine, and the Rhône, and other insignificant currents; but they never did, or could, pass Mr. Pitt's "Military Canal".'

The Martello Towers have not, as a whole, grown old as gracefully as the Canal. Many have disappeared altogether, and others have acquired a somewhat dingy and neglected appearance. But all the survivors are testimony of a dramatic period of history and as such they should be preserved. There is a particularly good series at Hythe which can be viewed from the end of the West Parade. Here, looking westwards, one sees a combination of fishing-boats drawn up on the beach and three of these sturdy round towers spaced out along the coast. Another Martello Tower, completely tamed and adapted to domestic use, is encountered amidst the houses of the sea-front, converted into a private residence and looking most delightful in its new role. Yet another once stood on the site now occupied by the Imperial Hotel. There are several at Dymchurch, one a fine monster almost astride the sea wall, and at Folkestone is Number One of the whole chain, still established on Copt Point. The Martellos stretched from Folkestone in Kent to Seaford in Sussex, and they were, like the Canal, never used for the purpose for which they were built. In fact, the whole series was not completed until after Nelson's victory had removed the threat of invasion.

The origin of the Martello Tower design, and of the name they bear, goes back to 1794, to the time when General Dundas led a British force of considerable size ashore in Corsica and received severe punishment from a garrison of only 22 men defending a small round tower at Mortella Point. When, at last, this intrepid little fort was taken, a British officer made a spelling error in his official report of the action. Instead of Mortella his message read Martello, and this has been the name given to these British forts ever since—for the lesson learnt in Corsica caused the design to be repeated all along the threat-ened English coast when Napoleon was building up his forces at Boulogne.

The design of the Towers provided a ground floor for stores and ammunition, while the upper storey accommodated a garrison of over 20 soldiers. On the top, shielded by a parapet, was a 24-pounder gun which could attack the enemy from any angle, and there were also openings for musket fire. Access to each tower was by means of a ladder which reached to an entrance high above the ground.

It is obvious, on such a smuggler-haunted coast as this,

11. Put to domestic use. This Martello Tower at Hythe has changed its character most successfully and provides an attractive home.

that once the Martello Towers were no longer garrisoned they would have some connection with the smuggling game— but no contraband-runner worth his salt would have selected so obvious a hiding-place for his cargoes. Instead, the Martellos became look-out posts from which the preventive men could spy on the furtive moon-lit activities of the beaches.

William Cobbett, in his *Rural Rides* (1821), dismisses the Martello Towers with scorn, but Cobbett was an inveterate Radical with a chip firmly entrenched on his shoulder. Anything achieved by what he called 'the Thing' (which nowadays would be referred to as 'the Establishment') was open to the full vent of his caustic pen. He derides the towers interminably, bemoaning their cost and seeming to ignore the dire national emergency during which they were erected. There is a vast difference between Cobbett's tiresomely obsessed denunciations of the Martello Towers and the wry humour of Barham's taunt at the Royal Military Canal.

Today the Martello Towers are a heritage for which most people have a strong affection, and any threat of demolition would be likely to cause a roar of protest. They are a familiar and rather curious part of the coastal scene, a legacy of perilous times, and yet another addition to the forts which, since the days of the Romans, have taken so many different sizes and shapes along this vulnerable shore.

4. The Castles of Saltwood and Lympne

There are two great castles near the Cinque Port of Hythe, both deeply entrenched in the history of the area. These are Saltwood Castle, on the northern outskirts of the town, and Lympne Castle, perched on the edge of the inland cliff above West Hythe. Both are of great antiquity and both belonged for centuries to Canterbury—Saltwood as a residence of the Archbishops, Lympne in a similar capacity for the Archdeacons. St. Thomas Becket resided at both, first as Archdeacon at Lympne and later as Archbishop at Saltwood. Both castles ultimately fell into disrepair, and were rescued from decay by private owners in comparatively recent times.

I will describe Saltwood first, for it is closer to the Cinque Port of Hythe than Lympne and practically on the fringe of the town. Unlike Lympne Castle it has not, to date, been open frequently to the public, and at the time of writing (1971) it is not open at all owing to structural work. Nevertheless, there is a gate marked 'Right of Way' which can be unlatched and a footpath followed which provides an excellent view from outside the walls.

It is easy, as one looks from this neighbouring meadow at the mighty walls and towers of Saltwood, to sense that on the fatal date of 28 December 1170, eve of the assassination of St. Thomas Becket, the castle looked very much as it does today. Here the four knights met to plot their evil deed—Reginald FitzUrse, Hugh de Moreville, William de Tracy and Richard le Breton. Henry II's ill-considered words 'Who will rid me of this turbulent priest?' had sent them hastening from his court in Normandy, where he was spending the Christmas season; and to ensure the complete secrecy of their journey the four knights divided into pairs, two arriving at Dover and two at Winchelsea.

The choice of the four knights' destination was appropriate, for the Castle was, at that time, in the hands of Becket's enemy,

12. Saltwood Castle. It was here that the four knights met on 28 December 1170, eve of the assassination of St. Thomas Becket in Canterbury Cathedral. Here they made final plans for the murder of the Archbishop.

de Broc—transfer of the Archbishop's residence by Henry II to de Broc having helped to fan the flames of the historic quarrel between the King and the inflexible Archbishop. The core of the quarrel was, of course, the question of division of secular and ecclesiastical jurisdiction, and Becket was adamant in his defence of the right of the Church to try clergy in its own courts; and the final rift was due to Becket's refusal to relent in any way on the question of his suspension and excommunication of the Archbishop of York and the Bishops of London and Salisbury.

On that fatal evening in December 1170, the four knights met, it is believed, in the great Norman Hall of the Castle, and according to legend they sat with extinguished candles so that none saw the other's face. On the morrow they rode to Canterbury, reaching the Archbishop's Palace and the Cathedral at the close of day. The rest of the story is well known: how, within the sacred walls of the Cathedral the murder was carried out; how FitzUrse aimed the first blow, but aimed badly; how this was followed by a second stroke from de Tracy, while a final massive slash from le Breton clove the upper part of the Archbishop's skull with such violence that the sword broke in two. The four knights left the body on the Cathedral floor, taking flight through the cloisters and away—into their unenviable place in the pages of history.

Saltwood Castle remained in the possession of the Crown until the reign of King John, when it was restored to Canterbury. The last Archbishop to occupy it was Cranmer, from whom it passed to Henry VIII and thence to his henchman, Thomas Cromwell. The Castle passed through the hands of many different families during the subsequent centuries, eventually becoming ruinous, and only in the nineteenth century was it restored, with great care, as a private residence. Today it is the family property of Lord Clark of Saltwood, the art historian. Lord Clark, after living there for nearly twenty years, decided the massive Castle was becoming too large for him, so early in 1971 he handed it over to his son.

In addition to the footpath view of the Castle, the parish church at Saltwood affords an impressive glimpse from the churchyard. The church should, in any case, be visited in its own right. It stands in a beautiful setting of meadows and stately trees, and its earliest features date from the first half of the twelfth century. The church then consisted of nave and chancel only, with no tower; the tower dates from about 1200. There are a number of good monumental brasses, among them an especially fine head and shoulders brass of 1370 commemorating Johannes Verien. Of the same period is the elaborately carved vestment chest—the front being original but the rest modern, for the death watch beetle demolished it. This is sad indeed, for the carved front is magnificent.

Lympne Castle, second of the great castles on the Hythe fringe, is massively built and superbly sited on the very edge

13. Lympne Castle viewed from the north, showing the entrance courtyard.

of the clifftop above Romney Marsh. It was for 800 years the
country residence of the Archdeacons of Canterbury, the most
famous of whom was St. Thomas Becket.

From the terrace of the Castle the grassy slopes swoop down
to the Marsh, with nothing to break the view but cattle
grazing on the hillside and groups of trees through which can
be glimpsed scattered grey masses of stone—all that remains of
the fort which guarded the Roman port. Here was Portus
Lemanis, a natural harbour of outstanding importance to the
Romans, and the fort was one of nine coastal strongholds
erected during the Roman occupation to defend the country
from Saxon raids. They were known as the Saxon Shore
Forts, and their commander bore the title of Count of the
Saxon Shore. At the top of the cliff, on the site where Lympne

14. Lympne Castle on its clifftop height. The Castle stands on the very edge of the escarpment which sweeps down to Romney Marsh.

Castle now stands, was a Roman watch tower; and during restoration of the Castle in 1905 the sole of a Roman shoe was found in a wall of the eastern tower.

Gradually, as has happened all along this treacherous coast, the sea assumed command and the harbour silted up. Today, instead of Roman galleys lying below the cliff, Romney Marsh stretches to the sea, while through the marshland the Royal Military Canal follows its unruffled course. Westward, in the misty distance, the arm of Dungeness stretches out into the sea, ever growing as the shingle steadily builds up. Along this coast, as the sea encroaches in one area it recedes and increases the shoreline in another, and at Dungeness the shingle contributes its quota of territory each year so that the land stretches ever farther out to sea. From Lympne the massive squat towers of the Dungeness nuclear power station are seen dimly on the promontory.

The dismembered Roman stones on the hillside below Lympne are now known as Stutfall Castle, the name being derived from Stout Wale, meaning strong fortress, as it was known when the Saxons, in their turn, used it as a defence post. Excavations were carried out here in 1851, and it has been proved from the buried foundations that the Roman fort covered an area of about 10 acres, that the walls were about 20 feet in height and 12 feet thick, and at the southern end of the eastern wall there was an entrance gateway of imposing proportions with towers on either side. Landslides, and the use of its stones for building purposes, brought the fort to its present state of decay, but the landslides, by burying the foundations, also aided their preservation so that archaeologists were able later to uncover them and establish the size and structure of the fort. After these excavations the foundations were again covered up.

Prior to the Conquest, a Saxon abbey stood on the Castle's clifftop site, and what became the Archdeacon's residence incorporated the former abbey's lodging house. Leland wrote in 1536 that 'as the church is now was sumtyme without fayle an abbay. The graves yet appeare yn the Chirch, and of the lodging of the Abbay be now converted ynto the Archdeacon's Howse.' The original conversion into the Archdeacon's residence, and the building of the Norman church which stands today close beside the Castle, were the work of Lanfranc, the first Norman Archbishop of Canterbury; for their construction it is said that stones from the surviving Roman structures at Lympne were used.

Lympne Castle remained the property of the Archdeacons of Canterbury until the latter part of the nineteenth century, though at times occupied by a number of non-ecclesiastical

tenants. It passed finally from the possession of the Arch-
deaconry when sold to Major Lawes of Dover, who did not
live here but installed a local farmer as tenant. Thus the
Castle's great days seemed over, and neglect and ruin set in
until, in 1905, Mr. Henry Tennant (brother of Margot, Lady
Asquith) bought it and set the Scottish architect, Sir Robert
Lorimer, to work on restoration. It was, incidentally, when the
Asquiths were staying at Lympne Castle, during the height of
the suffragette agitation, that a collection of determined
suffragettes climbed the ramparts and staged what would
today be described as a 'demo'.

From the time of Sir Robert Lorimer's restoration the Castle
has always been cared for, and from 1918 to 1947 it belonged
to Mr. Henry Beecham, brother of Sir Thomas Beecham. It
then passed to Mrs. Murray Payne, who sold it to the fifth and
present private owner, Mr. Harry Margary.

For visitors from the United States there is a special interest in the fact that Mr. Margary is the great-great-great-
grandson of the famous painter, Benjamin West (1738–1820),
who was born in Springfield, Pennsylvania, came to England
via Rome, and succeeded Sir Joshua Reynolds as President of
the Royal Academy of Arts in London. His best-known
painting, *Death of Wolfe,* is familiar to all. The cabinet where he
stored his sketches stands in the Great Hall at Lympne Castle,
and on it are the plain little eighteenth-century Wedgwood
pigment pots in which he used to mix his paints. A tale is
told of his childhood in Pennsylvania when, at a very early
age, he showed talent for drawing but was provided with
nothing more than pen and ink with which to develop his
skill; only when a group of Indians saw his sketches and
showed him how to produce the reds and yellows which they
used themselves was he able to try his hand at colour. With
indigo, which his mother provided, he was then able to mix
his paints. Even greater ingenuity was needed to acquire a
brush of the right texture, and the child managed this by
cutting fur from the cat's tail!

The Margary family are of French Huguenot origin, and their
ancestors came to this country as Protestant refugees following
the Massacre of St. Bartholomew, which took place in Paris

on the night of 24 August 1572. A much earlier ancestor came to this country in different mood; he was Aubyn de Marguerye, one of the captains in the expedition of 1295 led by the Compte d'Harcourt, who attacked Dover Castle but failed to take it, whereas Aubyn de Marguerye succeeded in capturing the town of Dover.

There are two towers at each extremity of Lympne Castle, and the Square Tower, beside the church, comprises the earliest part of the present building; it is of great strength, with walls five feet thick. At the west end of the Castle is the Great Tower of about 1360, its distinctive rounded section, with a newel staircase, having been added 60 years later.

The Great Hall, as in all early buildings, is the major room of the house; it has Tudor panelling throughout, with fireplace and chimneypiece of the same period. Also of interest is the old kitchen in the base of the Square (eastern) Tower, and on the western side the newel staircase in the Great Tower leads, via the Crown Post Chamber, to the parapet from which a superb view is gained.

There are, it seems, quite a number of ghosts at Lympne Castle, and the person who encountered them with any regularity was Mrs. Henry Beecham. One is a Roman soldier, who thumps up the steps of the eastern tower (which is, of course, on the site of the Roman watch tower) and gazes out seawards, always on guard for Saxon raiders. In his lifetime the sighting of raiders would cause an instant warning to be sent to the fort below, whereupon the Roman ships would set out to do battle with the Saxons in mid-Channel. The sea then came almost up to the Roman fort. There is a saying in Lympne that the ghostly Roman was so entranced with the view from his watch tower that he cannot leave.

Another ghost is a grave, sad-eyed priest who, according to Mrs. Beecham's description, used to look down into the Great Hall from the small slit window at the top of the eastern wall. He is believed to represent one of the seven Saxon priests who were living here at the time of the Domesday Survey of 1086. The Saxon clergy, as might be

15. Romney Marsh landscape from the terrace of Lympne Castle. Great boulders 300 feet below are all that remain of Stutfall Castle, the Saxon Shore Fort of the Romans. The Royal Military Canal is seen centre left.

expected, did not live very amicably with the Norman conquerors, and tradition says that the seven Saxon priests of Lympne were murdered. Whether this is true or not, the seven Saxon priests disappeared. Their existence was recorded in the Domesday Book, and four years later they were no more.

The third ghost is of the bird-phantom variety and sounds far more alarming than the sad-eyed priest and the vigilant Roman watchman. The body is that of an eagle, while the head is the skull of a man, and this unpleasant apparition is said to fly round and round the kingpost in the bedroom which belonged to the Archdeacon.

These are the ghost stories of Lympne Castle, and as good a trio as one is likely to find in any ancestral home. But I would say that there is no 'spooky' atmosphere there at all —just the pleasantest feeling of peace and friendliness.

5. To the Marsh by the Clifftop Road

The road which stretches from Lympne along the crest of the inland cliff is one that I find especially appealing. The scenery is gentle and lushly green, and always, where gaps appear in the trees on the seaward side, or where the trees give way to meadows, there are dramatic views over the flat, enigmatic land of the Marsh.

16. **The Shepway Cross** at Lympne. This cross is modern, having been erected in 1923, but it marks an ancient site—the traditional early meeting-place of the Court of Shepway of the Cinque Ports Confederation. There is a fine view over the Marsh from the Cross.

The Shepway Cross can be taken as a starting point for this route. The Cross itself is not old, dating only from 1923, but it is very impressive and marks an important site. The inscription records that it was erected 'in memory of the historic deeds of the Cinque Ports, on the ancient site of Shepway Cross, by William, Seventh Earl of Beauchamp, K.G., Lord Warden and Admiral, 1923'.

From the Shepway Cross, if the day is clear, the first of this upper road's fine views of Romney Marsh can be gained. For real atmospheric effect I like a mixture of dimness and clarity. If there is rain or a Marshland mist, then nothing will be visible at all; but neither is it ideal to have conditions of sparkling clarity, for then the sense of mystery is lost and the coastal buildings at Dymchurch stand out too clearly. With the right weather conditions the clifftop views over the Marsh are remarkable and compelling.

One road plunges down the hillside from the Cross and heads for Dymchurch and New Romney, but we shall visit these places later. At this point I am going to take the upper road, which passes the side-turning to the Castle and Norman church at Lympne, and then continues on the clifftop route to Court-at-Street. This small hamlet, and the neighbouring village of Aldington, provided the stage for the sixteenth-century story of Elizabeth Barton, known as 'The Maid of Kent' or 'The Holy Maid of Kent'.

Elizabeth Barton was a young servant girl in the household of Thomas Cobb of Aldington, Bailiff of Archbishop Warham of Canterbury (for much of the land in this neighbourhood belonged to Canterbury at this time). It appears that the girl suffered from some form of fit which, possibly combined with religious mania, caused her to make statements that were received with wonder and veneration. She was believed to be divinely inspired, and her pronouncements, made at a time when the country was in turmoil over Henry VIII's divorce from Catherine of Aragon and the break with Rome, gained special significance.

The parish priest of Aldington, Richard Masters, repeated her utterances to a monk named Bocking of Canterbury, who quickly spread the tidings to the country people in general, and to the Archbishop in particular. Archbishop Warham, much interested, issued instructions: 'Keep you diligent accompt of all her utterances; they come surely of God, and tell her that she is not to refuse or hide His goodness and works.' Thereupon it seems that Bocking and Masters set about using the girl for their own ends.

The ecclesiastical historian, John Strype (1643–1737)

17. **Chapel of the sixteenth-century 'Holy Maid of Kent'** at Court-at-Street. Today only a scanty remnant, overgrown with bushes and shrubs, survives on the hillside above the Marsh.

records, 'And to serve himself of this woman and her fits for his own benefit he (Masters), with one Dr. Bocking, a monk of Canterbury, directed her to say in one of her trances that she should never be well till she visited the image of Our Lady in a certain chapel in the said Masters' parish, called the Chapel in Court-at-Street; and that Our Lady had appeared to her and told her so; and that if she came on a certain day thither, she should be restored to health by miracle. This story, and the day of her resort unto the chapel, was studiously given out by the said parson and monk; so that at the appointed day there met 2,000 persons to see this maid, and the miracle to be wrought on her. Thither at the set time she came, and there, before them all, disfigured herself, and pretended her ecstasies.'

The fame of the 'Holy Maid of Kent' grew and caused so great a stir that it involved some of the greatest men of the day. Sir Thomas More and Bishop Fisher later suffered condemnation on the score of having withheld some of her sayings. She was transferred to Canterbury where, as a nun in the Benedictine convent of St. Sepulchre, she continued her revelations. Then, one ill-omened day, she began to pronounce against King Henry VIII and his divorce, maintaining that she had divine instructions to command him to amend his life, to destroy all that followed the new learning, and that, should he marry Anne Boleyn, God's vengeance would plague him. She went on to announce, with even greater audacity, that if the marriage went through the King would lose his kingdom.

This forecasting of wrath and doom so influenced the aged Archbishop Warham that he gained courage, at the last, to oppose the King's matrimonial plans. The amenable Cranmer succeeded him as Archbishop, and the King's marriage with Anne Boleyn was solemnized in January 1533.

At this point the King had had enough of Elizabeth Barton, and in 1533 Cranmer was given the task of examining the 'Holy Maid'. The result was a foregone conclusion. The girl confessed that she had never had visions at all, that all was feigned in order to gain worldly praise. Bocking, Masters and others of her associates were confined in the Tower of London where, on examination, they too confessed.

The story ends in April 1534 when the poor, deluded girl was led with her accomplices to Tyburn to pay the penalty for all her past acclamation and glory. Her words before execution were:

'Hither I am come to die; and I have not been only the cause of mine own death, which most justly I have deserved, but also I am the cause of the death of all those persons, which at this time here suffer. And yet, to say the truth, I am not so much to be blamed, considering that it was well known to these learned men that I was a poor wench, without learning; and therefore they might easily have perceived that the things that were done by me could proceed in no such sort; but their capacities and learning could right well judge from whence they proceeded, and that they were altogether feigned; but because the thing which I feigned was profitable to them, therefore they much praised me; and bore me in hand, that it was the Holy Ghost, and not I, that did them; and then I, being puffed up with their praises, fell into a certain pride and foolish fantasy with myself, and thought I might feign what I would; which thing hath brought me to this case; and for which now I cry God and the King's highness most heartily mercy, and desire you all, good people, to pray to God to have mercy on me, and on all them that here suffer with me.'

For a girl who was so simple, we are told, that she could not have made any of her religious pronouncements in her own right, this last scaffold speech seems a remarkably good piece of oratory. But it was a tragic end, and if Elizabeth Barton had to die one cannot help feeling glad that her mentor, Bocking, shared her fate. Masters was pardoned and returned to Aldington.*

So the chapel at Court-at-Street fell into final decay, though traces of it still stand, roofless and ruined, on the sloping side of the cliff above the Marsh. It is difficult to find, and the path down the hillside is overgrown and tends to be muddy. Nevertheless, those who persevere can still discover the chapel, and it is a strange thought, when the roofless walls of the little building come into view, to remember the processions and pilgrimages down the hillside in the heyday of Elizabeth Barton's renown. The chapel itself was already in existence before her time and, it seems, already in decay. According to

---

* *Author's note.* In 1971, when my description of the clifftop road was already written, an exhaustive study was published on the subject of Elizabeth Barton (*The Holy Maid of Kent* by Alan Neame). Mr. Neame is a descendant of Thomas Cobb, employer at Aldington of Elizabeth Barton, and he writes with a deep knowledge of his subject. His purpose is to vindicate the memory of the Holy Maid, whose story has undoubtedly, as he maintains, come down to us through the writings of those who favoured the Reformation and King Henry viii's divorce. I am not entirely converted to Mr. Neame's point of view, but anyone wishing to give Elizabeth Barton a fair hearing should read this book.

18. Spring scene in the churchyard at Aldington, where the Romney Marsh sheep and their lambs seem at home among the gravestones.

Hasted, the chapel 'usually called the Chapel of Our Lady of Court-at-Street from its being dedicated to the Blessed Virgin Mary, was built for the use of the inhabitants of the adjoining hamlet, and when it fell into decay this chapel most probably became neglected insomuch that in King Henry VIII's reign it seems to have been mostly used for a hermit to dwell in'.

There is a rough footpath down the hillside through private farmland, only accessible with the permission of the owners of Manor Farm, Mr. and Mrs. Duthoit. Mrs. Duthoit told me that there used to be a spring-fed pool beside the chapel, in which the pilgrims would wash before entering, and that in her grandparents' day this was still crystal clear. Today it is weed-grown and hardly visible as a pool at all.

A short distance from Court-at-Street the village of Alding-ton is reached, and the fine tower of its church is visible from afar as one approaches. Goldwell Hall, where Elizabeth Barton was employed as a servant girl by Thomas Cobb, still survives, though much altered since her time.

This peaceful village is a place where one would have expected little to happen, but in addition to the drama already related the names of two famous men of the sixteenth century are to be found in the church's list of rectors. One was the celebrated Dutch scholar Desiderius Erasmus, to whom Archbishop Warham granted the benefice in 1511. He remained in Aldington for about one year and then resigned, suggesting that as he was unable to preach in English there was little point in staying! The other famous rector was the great English scholar and physician, Thomas Linacre, who was the Greek tutor of Sir Thomas More and founder of the Royal College of Physicians.

It was springtime when I was last in Aldington and the whole village seemed bathed in calm and dappled sunshine. Farm buildings with deep, mellow roofs led up to St. Martin's Church, and in the churchyard the woolly Romney Marsh sheep, with their considerably whiter lambs, were nibbling among the gravestones. The church dates, in the main, from the twelfth to the sixteenth centuries.

Although the door is usually locked the key is available at the neighbouring farm, approached by a gate from the church-yard. The fourteenth-century choir stalls alone are ample reward for fetching the key, for they are considered to be among the finest in any church in Kent, with boldly-carved misericords in a remarkable state of preservation. It is sug-gested that the existence of such choir stalls in a quiet village church is due to the former presence of a palace of the Arch-bishops of Canterbury which once stood to the east of St. Martin's.

Another extremely interesting woodcarving dominates the pulpit and depicts the theme of the Pelican in her Piety, much favoured in medieval carving. The pelican is shown feeding her fledgelings with blood from her own breast and thus bringing them back to life after their waywardness had caused her to kill them—symbolizing man's redemption through the blood of Christ. This carving dates from the late fifteenth or early sixteenth century and had a narrow escape from destruction; it came to light in the last century, covered with whitewash, in a farmhouse near by.

A glass case beside the font contains the musical instruments that were used in the former minstrel's gallery in the tower—an oboe, a flute, and a bassoon. The bassoon, according to the note beside it, is pitched in the key of 'C' to accompany vocal music, and the villagers' name for it was 'the Horse's Leg'. A 'Breeches' Bible is preserved here. In this version Genesis III, 7, reads: 'Then the eyes of them both were opened and they knew they were naked, and they sewed figge-leaves together, and made themselves breeches' (instead of aprons).

Between Aldington and Bonnington on this upper road there are some grand views over the Marsh, and then the road becomes thickly wooded as it descends steeply to a lower level. At Bonnington there is a beautiful little church which should not be missed, though it hides itself away most elus-ively. It is about a mile from the village, on the Bonnington to Newchurch road, and stands shyly among trees, with the Royal Military Canal flowing below. The Canal is in its most peaceful mood here, seeming almost in league with the church in its wish to hide away, and sharing its banks only with clusters of Romney Marsh sheep and their lambs.

Bonnington church is dedicated to St. Rumwold, identified in the notes within the church with St. Rumwald, a seventh-century child saint born in King's Sutton, Northamptonshire. His legendary history is that he lived for only three days, but, having the miraculous power of speech, he preached at Brackley on the second day of his very limited existence. The church is of Norman origin, with a fourteenth-century roof of tie-beam and king-post construction. The font is Norman, of a simple cauldron shape with an elegant Jacobean cover—the latter widely different in style and date from the font, but very attractive.

Bilsington, the next village on the Lympne to Hamstreet road, has a church which does not attempt to hide itself as you

19. Close to Bonnington Church the Royal Military Canal flows by—its waters, and the Romney Marsh sheep on its banks, forming a characteristically peaceful Marshland scene.

draw near, yet once you are *in* Bilsington it disappears. The approach, when eventually discovered, is down a tiny lane that seems to be leading only to farm buildings. But at the end of the lane is the church, ard if you visit it at the beginning of May the trees in the churchyard will be bursting into blossom, and the sheep and their lambs, as at Aldington, will be cropping the grass and looking in sole possession. This is a church of great antiquity, sadly over-restored in the nineteenth century; but nothing the Victorians could do succeeded in destroying the sense of calm and long centuries of worship which it conveys. It has the text boards so characteristic of the churches of the Marsh area, and an imposing rendering of the Royal

Arms (George III, 1774) over the chancel arch. There are some scanty but interesting remains of old glass.

Nothing could be more peaceful than Bilsington Church, and the only sound when I was there was the song of the birds and the plaintive baa-ing of the sheep. In the churchyard one of the bells hangs, almost at ground level, beneath a little lych gate roof, erected to protect it. It cannot be rung, for it is cracked, and I was told by some parishioners who came to tend a grave that when it fell it was given this little roofed support rather than that it should be discarded. Near by I noticed a grave whose inscription told the tale of a family of children who, like Peter Pan, never grew up. They were: Thomas Law, died 1865, aged 6 weeks; Benjamin Daniel Law, died 1867, aged 7 weeks; Elizabeth Jane Law, died 1868, aged 13 years; Fanny Laura Law, died 1868, aged 10 years; Julia Maria Law, died 1869, aged 4 years. This sad grave should, I felt, have been at Bonnington, in the graveyard of the church dedicated to the little three-days-old saint, rather than at Bilsington.

There was a Priory of Austin Canons at Bilsington, founded in 1253, but this was surrendered to the Crown on Henry VIII's dissolution of the monasteries and was put to secular use, the old building eventually becoming incorporated in a farmhouse. The priory estate was purchased in 1825 by Sir William Richard Cosway, who is commemorated by the curious obelisk which stands gauntly in the middle of a meadow near the church and completely mystifies most approaching motorists.

The story of Sir William Cosway is this: although he did not take up residence in the village he took a very active interest in its affairs and as an advocate of the Reform Bill he was keenly aware of the distress of the farm labourers whose wages were desperately low. His concern took practical form, for in 1830 it is recorded that he lent the sum of £150 to enable four Bilsington families to emigrate to America. Today £150 would not go very far, but in 1830 it was possible to sail from Rye Harbour to New York for £8 5s. (or £8·25). In 1833 Sir William was again helping the villagers by the construction of a small school for the education of their children. Then, on 10 June 1834, he was killed when the London to Brighton 'Criterion' coach overturned as it was leaving the Borough in London. The obelisk, 52 feet in height, was erected one year later, and it was repaired in both 1893 and 1940 with the aid of funds contributed by the villagers.

After Bilsington comes Ruckinge, where the church's massively built Norman tower stands close beside the road; mercifully, the ornamentation of the Norman south doorway has not been glossed over by Victorian restoration but has been allowed to moulder in aged dignity.

This is the end of the upper road, and it is, in fact, no longer 'upper' at all at this stage. At Bonnington, Bilsington, Ruckinge or Hamstreet there are roads leading away southwards and heading for the Marsh itself.

But before exploring the Marsh there is another fringe area which can be combined with the upper road. This is the Isle of Oxney, once an island in the true sense of the word and now a long, low ridge of land which seems to be heaving itself upwards from the Rother Levels like a somnolent whale. The Isle of Oxney lies between Stone-in-Oxney to the east and Wittersham to the west, and it still retains something of that island character owing to a framework of waterways, notably the river Rother to the south, and eastwards the Royal Military Canal on its route from Appledore to Rye.

At Stone, high above the marshland, stands St. Mary's Church, its sturdy fifteenth-century tower rising to a height of over 60 feet. Roses are trained along the rustic fence which fronts the church, and behind is a shrubbery planted to commemorate the Festival of Britain of 1951. There are snowdrops to welcome the approach of spring, then primroses, daffodils and flowering shrubs.

The church which this one replaced in the fifteenth century was destroyed by fire in 1464, and in the nineteenth century restoration played its part in a bit of destruction too—removing the gallery, pews and chancel stalls, and renewing the east windows. In this instance, however, the results of restoration were not altogether bad, for during the work two windows were discovered above the chancel arch, as were the rood beam apertures. Among the list of rectors (starting in 1287) appears the name of William Gostling (1753), whose father had a bass voice so rich that Purcell wrote his anthem, *They that go down to the sea in ships*, in order that it should be given full scope.

One item in the church has aroused widespread interest. This is the ancient stone which stands beneath the tower and bears on the front a much-weathered portrayal of a bull—from which it has been deduced that it was an altar dedicated to the Roman God Mithras. It was this suggestion of pagan origin which caused the stone to endure a number of damaging adventures, for it was not considered suitable for a Christian church. It became (appropriately enough, we have to admit) a horse block at the Black Ox Inn, from which hard service it was retrieved by the rich bass's son, the Rev. William Gostling. He had it restored—but then left it to weather in his garden! Now, at last, it is being adequately cared for and, pagan or not, is safely installed in the church at Stone-in-Oxney.

This Mithras stone is not the only unexpected discovery in St. Mary's for close beside it, beneath the tower, are the fossilized bones of an iguanodon and the scales of a fish, both found in the quarry at Stone in 1935. The British Museum identified the bones as nine tail vertebrae, some portions of ribs, and the distal end of a bone of the hind limb, forming the ankle joint. The note beside these bones in the church helpfully explains that the iguanodon was a dinosaur which flourished in the Mesozoic era and became extinct about 70,000,000 years ago. They were the largest animals that ever walked on earth, were cold-blooded and slow-moving, with smaller brains and less intelligence than the warm-blooded mammals that succeeded them. The iguanodon was a land animal which stood two-legged like a kangaroo. Its three-toed footprints have been found in the Wealdon rocks of Sussex. The fish scales were identified as part of a lepidotus. All this excellent information was typed out beside the exhibits in Stone-in-Oxney Church—and how much more interesting it is to study such exhibits when regaled with full details in this way!

From Stone-in-Oxney it is only a short distance to Small-hythe, a rural one-street village which once boasted a busy shipyard and quays on the tidal river Rother—almost impossible to imagine today. Smallhythe was the port for Tenterden (two miles away) which, as a Corporate Member of Rye, received Cinque Port privileges. Even as late as Henry VIII's reign an important warship was built at Smallhythe for the royal fleet and the King came personally to inspect its progress. By the end of the sixteenth century, however, the silting-up process had made it possible for only the smallest craft to sail to Smallhythe, and today, instead of shipyards and quays, we see only the green meadows and agricultural life to which the area turned when it ceased to be a port.

The dominating personality of Smallhythe was (and still is, long after her death) Dame Ellen Terry, the great actress who made Smallhythe Place her country home for just under 30 years. This charming old black and white half-timbered house dates from about 1480 and was the Port House, or harbourmaster's house, in the days of the shipbuilding yards. When the sea receded and Smallhythe's port days were over the house became known, simply, as The Farm. This is the name by which Ellen Terry always referred to it. Here she was at her happiest, completely relaxed, and enjoying the carefree gatherings of her family. Here she died on 21 July 1928.

The whole area around Smallhythe Place is very closely connected with Ellen Terry for she bought the entire estate in 1899. This consisted of Smallhythe Place itself, Yew Tree Cottage opposite, the half-timbered Priest's House beside the church, and about 40 acres of land. Her daughter, Edith Craig, lived in the Priest's House, and it was Edith Craig who gave Smallhythe Place to the National Trust in 1939 as a memorial to her mother.

It is the most perfect memorial to Ellen Terry that could be imagined, for the house still retains so much of its old informal atmosphere—possibly because her daughter was for years responsible for its care and the arrangement of the rooms. This meant that there was little rearrangement, and everything that had built up the warmth and affection of this home in Ellen Terry's time was retained without creating the sense of preservation so often found in a museum. Ellen Terry's was an unforgettable personality, and she is still spoken of with affection in neighbouring Winchelsea and Rye, but most of all

20. **Smallhythe Place,** country home for nearly 30 years of the great actress Dame Ellen Terry, and now the Ellen Terry Memorial Museum. Smallhythe was once the busy port of Tenterden, Corporate Member of Rye; but the silting up of the tidal river Rother eventually left both Smallhythe and Tenterden far inland.

in Smallhythe. Her bedroom has remained unchanged since she died, and the dining-room still seems to reflect the gaiety of those family gatherings in the later years of her life. In her copy of Thomas à Kempis' *Imitation of Christ* she wrote, 'No funeral gloom, my dears, when I am gone', and there has never been any gloom at Smallhythe Place.

This is a house for all students of the history of the theatre to visit. There is the Terry Room with mementoes and souvenirs collected by all the members of this theatrical family, from the ivory stick carried by Dame Ellen's brother, Fred Terry, in his most famous role *The Scarlet Pimpernel*, to the dagger used by Sir John Gielgud, her great-nephew, in *Hamlet*.

In the Dining-Room is a theatrical collection which includes relics and portraits of such past giants of the stage as David Garrick, Sarah Siddons, Sarah Bernhardt, Rachel, Eleanora Duse . . . The Lyceum Room is devoted to the long acting partnership of 24 years between Ellen Terry and Sir Henry Irving, and in the Costume Room are some of the costumes worn by Ellen Terry, beautifully displayed and still in perfect condition. One, worn as Hiordes in *The Vikings* in 1903, is of special interest, for it was designed by her son, Gordon Craig, and made by her daughter, Edith.

Gordon Craig, writer, artist and theatrical designer, became as great a name in the world of the theatre as his mother, but he achieved his fame on the Continent and in America rather than in this country. I well remember seeing him in 1962, sitting at a café table in Vence in the south of France, playing Patience—a habit to which the whole Terry family was addicted. He was a grand old man with a face in the Leonardo da Vinci mould—a face that would be a gift to any portrait painter. Every now and then someone would come and speak to him, with an air of deference, and he would listen with polite courtesy—yet with one eye on the cards and an obvious wish to keep to the game. Then his daughter joined him and away they went, arm-in-arm; a striking figure, he disappeared into the distance, his long cloak sweeping behind him, his mane of white hair blowing in the wind and adding to his general air of distinction. Now he too is dead. After Ellen Terry's death at Smallhythe Place, innumerable packs of Patience cards were found stowed away all over the house.

The Church of St. John the Baptist at Smallhythe is a most unexpected structure at a first glance, and seems totally un-suited to its surroundings. It was built in 1514 following a fire which demolished most of the hamlet of Smallhythe, and instead of taking the traditional English church form of the period it emerged as a red-brick building of a design strongly reflecting the Dutch influence. In particular, this is revealed in the stepped gables of the West Front. In this church Ellen Terry's funeral service was conducted. Beside it is the half-timbered Priest's House which became her daughter's home.

From Smallhythe it is only a comparatively short journey to Rye and Winchelsea, but as the whole clifftop road has served as an introduction to the Marsh I will leave the two 'Antient Towns' until later, for this seems the moment to explore the Marsh itself.

6. The Marsh Today and Dungeness

I have already described how the true Romney Marsh is the land east of the site of the Rhee Wall; how the other Marshes, Walland and Denge, lie to the west of the Wall as far as the Kent–Sussex border; and how the Sussex marshland stretching to Rye is named the Guldeford Level. This is the land which the Rev. Richard Barham in his *Ingoldsby Legends* describes as the fifth quarter of the globe. Its attraction cannot be detected at a glance, and those who look at its flat, secretive expanses with unseeing eyes, merely regarding it as an area to motor through at speed, will never catch a glimpse of its hidden spirit at all.

It is often misty in this dyke-intersected countryside and in its approaches, but this does not detract from its appeal. William Cobbett, in his *Rural Rides,* writes of his approach to the Marsh as he comes from Tenterden, and his account could equally well have been written today instead of 150 years ago: 'From Tenterden I set off at five o'clock, and got to Appledore after a most delightful ride, the high land upon my right, and the low land on my left. The fog was so thick and white along some of the low land that I should have taken it for water, if the little hills and trees had not risen up through it here and there.'

Although this marshland retains a quite different character from anywhere else, changes have necessarily come, especially during the past 50 years. Some are good, some bad—and the transformation of the Dymchurch coastline by the holiday trade cannot be considered an asset by anyone with a love of the marshland scene. On the other hand, more efficient drainage and the introduction of electricity have made the Marsh a healthier and more comfortable place to live in. The pylons and telegraph wires do disturb the vista, but who would deprive the Marshlanders of their benefits?

In the old days, when this was true marshland and frequently

D

21. Romney Marsh sheep beside a dyke in the Marsh. This famous breed is also known by the alternative title of Kent sheep, and is completely acclimatized to the weather conditions and pastures of the Marsh.

flooded, 'the ague'—probably a form of malaria—was prevalent. It was known among the people of the Marsh as 'Old Johnny', and was kept at bay (or so they hoped) by the wearing of a charm hung from a cord round the neck which bore the words:

> Ague, I thee defy.
> Three days shiver,
> Three days shake,
> Make me well for Jesu's sake.

There is another ague charm which was used in other parts of the country, and although not a Marshland custom I think it is sufficiently amusing to relate. In this case the verse had to be recited up the chimney:

> Tremble and go!
> First day shiver and burn.
> Tremble and quake!
> Second day shiver and learn.
> Tremble and die!
> Third day never return.

So, with the disappearance of 'Old Johnny', all changes cannot be looked at askance.

It is just as well, too, that more efficient drainage has prevented the little marshland church at Fairfield from floating in periods of flood like a ship at sea—however picturesquely forlorn it used to look when this happened. Nevertheless, the sea level, the dykes and the sea wall still dominate most people's thoughts, and when I went into the church at Appledore one Sunday morning last year the topic of conversation, prior to the service, was just the same as it might have been centuries ago. 'The waters are rising' were the words I heard.

Sheep farming has, for centuries, been an integral part of the life of the Marsh, and it still is, although the great fertility of the soil is causing more and more of the grazing land to be lost to the plough. Certain areas have long been under cultivation, however, and when William Cobbett came to Old Romney in the 1820's his ever-active pen recorded that 'they reap the wheat here nearly two feet from the ground; and even then they cut it three feet long! I never saw corn like this before . . . They have here about eight hundred large, very large, sheaves to an acre.'

Despite the plough, and the buildings on the coastal fringe, this countryside remains fundamentally unchanged, a land of twisting dykes and twisting lanes—perfectly constructed for the smugglers of old to outwit the preventive men, and equally well constructed for the newcomer to get lost in today. It seems so easy, on seeing a map of the marshland churches, to decide which one to visit in an afternoon, and it is equally easy, after so confident a start, to find oneself in a quite different section of the Marsh to the part intended. This seems absurd, for the inland cliff, with Lympne Castle as a landmark on its height, is an easily visible northern boundary; and the tall, lonely churches should be easily sighted in the level Marsh. But these erratic lanes can lead you towards your target and then turn away again like a will-o'-the wisp, and the occasional broken signpost is no help at all.

Being a stranger to the Marsh myself (you cannot be anything else unless you were born and bred there), I have devised an admirable system for visiting the marshland churches and villages without becoming too exasperated. The scheme is simplicity itself, and benefits from a pleasant element of the unexpected. You have your list of churches and places you wish to see. Therefore you set out, let us say, by descending the cliff from the Shepway Cross and deciding to visit Burmarsh. You follow the first signpost to Burmarsh and find yourself in Newchurch instead. This sort of thing happens all the time, but what matter—you wanted to see Newchurch anyway. Similarly, you search for the scanty ruins of Hope, and although they evade you with persistent elusiveness, you encounter with inevitable frequency the lone arch of Midley. In this way you learn the twisting byways of the Marsh by degrees, eventually reaching all the places you set out to find—even if the order is different. It is not, of course, a touring system for the planner, but most pleasant for the rest of us.

Everywhere, where the plough has not encroached, the Romney Marsh sheep are grazing, and in order to discover more about this famous local breed I went to see Mr. Claude Paine of Lydd, an important sheep farmer and landowner of the Marsh, whose family have lived and farmed there for about 200 years. He told me much about the sheep, and much else concerning the Marsh.

The breed, sometimes referred to by the alternative title of Kent sheep, has been in the Marsh for centuries and is completely acclimatized to its weather conditions and pastures. Other breeds do not weather so well in this flat, low-lying countryside, for they are used to uplands and most of the Marsh is below sea level. The Romney Marsh sheep have white faces and a heavy fleece, and being big-framed sheep they are a double-purpose animal, excellently suited for both wool and meat. Fashions change in sheep rearing as in everything else, Mr Paine told me, and whereas in the old days the sheep had to be fattened for the butcher, this no longer applies. No one wants fat on meat today, and it so happens that the Romney Marsh sheep are well suited to this fashion, for they do not easily run to fat. A Romney Marsh ewe is good for grazing purposes, and as an export these hardy sheep have been introduced to many distant lands. In fact, some of the first sheep in Australia were shipped over from the Lydd area of the Marsh.

Film-goers with long memories will recall the delightful film version of *Joanna Godden*, Sheila Kaye-Smith's well-known novel of the Marsh. Part of this film was shot on Mr. Paine's land, his sheep and horses playing their part in the marshland scenes. The hero and heroine were played by Googie Withers and John McCallum, and the romance they were enacting became a romance in real life, for they married and their daughter was named Joanna in memory of the marshland film through which they met. Since then Googie Withers and John McCallum have made their life in Australia (it was his homeland), and I think that many Australians, on a visit to Britain, may find special interest in knowing that this is the countryside of the Joanna Godden novel and of the film which brought these two Australian personalities together.

Change does not come readily to the true people of the Marsh, but many young men of good shepherding stock were forced to drift away during the bad sheepfarming years between the wars. This caused a shortage of shepherds and shearers for, as Mr. Paine said, a man becomes a shepherd in youth or not at all. Earlier, during the first decade of the century, resentment and prejudice greeted the introduction of the first shearing machines, but these did, by degrees, replace hand shearing.

From Romney Marsh sheep one's mind turns to that full-throated creature, the 'Marsh Frog', who in the courting season makes the marshland echo with his croaking; he barks with a harsh 'warck-warck' sound, whereas the female gives voice on a more soothing and seductive note.

Mr. Paine related to me the story of this frog and the introduction, for better or for worse, of the species to the Marsh in 1935. The culprit was, it seems, the wife of the late E. P. Smith, Member of Parliament for Ashford and playwright (he was the author of *The Shop at Sly Corner*). E. P. Smith's birthday was at hand, and Mrs. Smith wanted to give him a surprise—so she went to London with the idea of obtaining some French frogs of the edible variety to put in their garden

Eric Hosking.

22. The Marsh Frog, *rana ridibunda,* is the Hungarian frog. Six pairs were brought to Stone-in-Oxney in 1935, and the species has since spread all over the Marsh.

pond. She was unlucky, for the French frogs were unobtainable, and all she could get were the large Hungarian (Rana Ridibunda) frogs. She brought six pairs home in the train from Charing Cross and put them into the pond in their garden at Stone—the Stone-in-Oxney where I described the church's Roman Mithras altar and the fossilized dinosaur's bones; so worse things than dinosaur's bones have come from Stone, for this large and noisy frog was not satisfied to stay in the Smiths' pond. The next year the original dozen and their offspring sallied forth to a nearby dyke, and the species then spread by about a mile every year until it covered the Marsh;

in doing so, it has almost exterminated the little yellow water frog which was natural to the area.

Although the native frog of the Marsh has succumbed to this large and bullying interloper, the Marsh toads have held their own and there is one, in particular—living in a drain-gulley in the path before Mr. Paine's front door—that has achieved fame on television! This narrow gully is so constricted that he has to deflate in order to emerge at all, but it is a domicile so much to his liking that he has been there for years. His name is Toby, and his special edible delicacy is wood lice, a dish which the Paine grandchildren—and grandfather, too—serve up for him. Toby's appetite for wood lice is so insatiable that they set traps and present a squirming bowl to the toad, who watches, eyes gleaming in anticipation, from his drain. The wood lice are then tipped into the narrow aperture, and as they sometimes, like hedgehogs, keep still in danger, Toby sits watching them with a hypnotic stare; he will not touch them unless they move. Then, when one victim thinks it has remained still long enough and makes a bid for freedom, out comes his tongue, a good two inches in length, and the luckless wood louse disappears. This sounds a revolting little story, but one cannot get too emotional about the fate of wood lice.

Toby has, in fact, inhabited the drain for about six or seven years, and on one occasion he returned from a period of wandering with a baby frog on his back; but this disappeared and one can only conjecture that either Toby felt like a change of diet or junior had an urge for wider horizons than the drain.

On the occasion of Toby's television appearance he was in a particularly evasive mood, and the cameramen became stiff and exhausted from the ordeal of crouching in wait for Toby to deflate and emerge. The toad, of course, knew all about it and just didn't oblige. Only after several hours did he finally deflate and carry on with his tele-performance—which, with judicious cutting, made him appear the most willing and sociable toad in the world.

Sad to say, I did not see Toby. He was out courting, and Mr. Paine told me that the male toad can rival the Marsh Frog for noise at this season. Long may Toby live—and in this respect he is possibly a wise old toad in his choice of a home, for chemical sprays are far from beneficial to wild life today. So Toby stays in his drain, free from sprays, and waxing fat and healthy on a wholesome diet of wood lice.

Bird life in the Marsh tends to be quite different in species to those found north of the Royal Military Canal. This does not mean that the Canal forms an invincible barrier but merely that it happens to be the northern boundary of the Marsh; thus, woodland and garden birds remain to the north of the Canal line, whereas the species that favour a more watery habitat are naturally found in the marshland to the south. The plough, with resultant crops of barley and potatoes instead of grazing land, has also resulted in a different bird population. Herons, which nest in the tops of trees, do not breed in the Marsh, but since they feed in a water area they are frequently seen there—always, of course, beside the water of the dykes.

Mr. Bob Scott, Warden of the Royal Society for the Protection of Birds' reserve at Dungeness, gave me a great deal of valuable information about the bird life of the Marsh. The R.S.P.B. first became interested in the Dungeness area from the point of view of its bird life at the beginning of the century, but it was not until the inter-war period that it first acquired land there. Then the project went into suspension during the Second World War, for the army requisitioned the whole of Dungeness.

At this time Pett Level, near Winchelsea, was flooded for defence purposes, and many birds unusual to the district were attracted there; but now, with the Pett Level dry land again, most of them have departed. There is, in the Rye Museum, a display case containing stuffed examples of some of the birds which came to the flooded Pett Level during those war years. In 1970 a new Nature Reserve was opened on this section of coast by the Sussex Naturalists' Trust, stretching from the Rother mouth at Rye harbour to Winchelsea beach. The Dungeness R.S.P.B. Bird Reserve reopened in its present form in 1952.

According to Mr. Scott very few bird species are absolutely peculiar to the Marsh. Drainage has lessened flooding, and the birds that used to be here have sought another, more watery, habitat. But where the true marshland conditions remain there are still species such as Reed Warblers, Sedge Warblers, Redshanks and Yellow Wagtails. To a great extent, today, the birds are the species that favour an agricultural rather than a marshland area, and another factor which is affecting the bird life of the Marsh is the expansion of home building in such places as Dymchurch, New Romney and

Eric Hosking.

23. Heron in flight. Herons are often seen beside the dykes of the Marsh.

Lydd, where garden shrubs and hedges are encouraging an increasing number of non-Marsh birds. Among these are the Spotted Flycatcher and the Chaffinch, while the birds associated with the gardens of London, such as the Blackbird and the Song Thrush, are tending to become far more apparent. They were in the Marsh originally, but only in isolated pockets of woodland or hawthorn hedges.

One or two species of the Dungeness birds are specially interesting. For instance, the shingle area of Dungeness is the only place in England (but not in Britain) where the Common Gull nests regularly. The bird is seen frequently in winter all over England, but it comes to Dungeness to nest. I learned from Mr. Scott that there is only one Common Gull (so named), although there are five common gulls (the species

24. One of the series of Dungeness lighthouses whose replacement from time to time has been made necessary by the receding sea. This is the 1792 Samuel Wyatt lighthouse, portrayed in an old print by Daniell. It depicts the Christmas Day occasion when the lighthouse was struck by lightning, but the

tower was so powerfully built that little damage resulted. Wyatt's lighthouse was demolished in 1904 and was superseded, in turn, by two further versions, both of which stand on the Dungeness shingle today. The latest, built in 1961, sheds a light of 300,000 candlepower intensity.

in general)—a piece of information which I am passing on for the benefit of readers who, like myself, are a bit vague on gulls.

This Dungeness stretch of coast has been recognized for a number of years as an ideal place for watching and studying bird migration; it is a promontory on the south-east corner of Britain, and it is relatively quiet. Mr. Scott emphasized that any such area, suitably placed, with bird watchers regularly recording migrants each day over a period of years, would be bound to encounter some rare species. Among examples at Dungeness, for instance, have been the slate-coloured Junco from North America, recorded in 1960, and the Radde's Warbler, which comes from South-East Asia (1962). A rarity recorded in the Marsh was the Snowy Owl, found near Brookland in 1965—the largest of the owls seen in this country.

Dungeness itself is no beauty spot, but it is most remarkable geologically. In addition, there is a strange appeal about it. The great nuclear power station is intimidating and not one's idea of seaside architecture, but then, Dungeness is not one's idea of a seaside resort anyway. There is shingle, shingle everywhere, and it is dry, rattling shingle at that. Yet out of this stony wilderness grass grows in sparse clumps, bushes of gorse produce a flash of colour in their season, while an occasional foxglove rears its purple head as if in surprise that it should have rooted strongly enough to rise up and look around. Here, too, are clumps of the valerian which grows so luxuriantly in the stone walls of Devon and Cornwall. How these hardy plants succeed in finding nourishment in the Dungeness shingle is difficult to understand, but there they are, and apparently liking it.

It is only when you know its story that this no-man's-land of shingle takes on a curious fascination. You look at the shoreline, and you know that could you return in 100 years' time it would be differently placed to where you see it now; and you look back at the old lighthouse, stranded inland, and realize that this was, not so very long ago, beside the sea. A soaring and slim new version has been built beside the present seashore, but the former is, in my eyes at any rate, the more majestic. These two lighthouses provide one of the best clues to the changing shoreline of Dungeness.

The history of the Dungeness lighthouses is fascinating. The first light for aiding shipping was erected in 1615 and consisted of a tower with an open coal fire at the top. This dwindled to a candle-lit warning when transportation of coal became difficult, but the candles cannot have offered much service to shipping. By 1635 this tower was no longer on the water's edge, so it was demolished and another constructed, but this, in its turn, was deserted by the receding sea. Only in 1792 was a really efficient lighthouse built and then, at last, the ineffectual coal fire was abandoned. Built by Samuel Wyatt, the design was similar to the Eddystone lighthouse; it rose to a height of 116 feet and was first of all lit by oil, followed by the installation of electric light in 1862. Wyatt's tower was eventually, like the others, left inland, so it was replaced at the beginning of the century by what is today termed the old lighthouse. The latest one was erected in 1961, the main light giving a 300,000 candle-power intensity with a range of 17 miles on a clear night. It was the narrowness of the Channel between the lighthouses of Dungeness and Cap Gris Nez in France that inspired George Meredith's lines, 'Where Gris Nez winks at Dungeness, across the ruffled strip of salt.'

One of the most prominent features of the Dungeness shore is the life-boat station, and this has a splendid record of bravery and dauntless rescues to its credit. One special feature is that it is a real family affair, presided over by two families, the Oillers and the Tarts. The Tarts' ancestors arrived in a fishing-boat from the France of the French Revolution, and the Oillers hailed from Cornwall. Until comparatively recently two women of the former family were launchers of the life-boats. In an emergency women still help to launch the life-boats at Dungeness, the only life-boat station in the country (at the time of writing, at any rate) where this applies.

This promontory of Dungeness is the outpost of the Marsh, and a stern one indeed; but it is very well worth a visit— especially in the little train. Dungeness forms part of the Borough of Lydd, and this is a member of the Cinque Ports Confederation as a Corporate Member of New Romney. But I shall describe Lydd separately in another chapter.

7. Smugglers and Their Hiding-Places

Two factors influenced for centuries the lives and tempera-
ment of the people of the Cinque Ports and the Marsh—the
introduction of a permanent Customs system and the activities
of the press gang. The first encouraged lawlessness and the
smuggler, the second resulted in desperate hardship for the
families whose menfolk were seized forcibly in time of war
to man the royal fleet. The smugglers developed a network of
hiding-places in houses, tunnels and caves where they stored
their contraband, pending its conveyance by heavily laden
ponies to secret destinations; and these 'hides' also served as
places of concealment from the press gang.

The seamen of the coastal area were in special danger of
impressment, for these were the men whom the press gang
were after—the men whose lives had been spent in fishing
and sailing and who had learnt to handle a boat almost as
soon as they could walk. There were no provisions for the
families of men removed in this way, and a wife could be
left penniless without even being told what had happened to
the husband who did not return.

The press gang did not hesitate to use violence in their
kidnapping, and Thackeray gives as good an account as any in
his last and unfinished novel, *Denis Duval*. The scene is set
in Winchelsea at a time when both smuggling and the press
gang were rampant, and here is Denis's description of the
incident:

'I was sauntering homewards, lost in happy thoughts,
when something occurred which at once decided the whole
of my after-life. This something was a blow with a bludgeon
across my ear and temple which sent me to the ground
utterly insensible. I remember half a dozen men darkling
in an alley by which I had to pass, then a scuffle and an oath
or two, and a voice crying "Give it him, curse him!" and

25. Smugglers at work.

then I was down on the pavement as flat and lifeless as the flags on which I lay. When I woke up, I was almost blinded with blood; I was in a covered cart with a few more groaning wretches; and when I uttered a moan, a brutal voice growled out with many oaths an instant order to be silent, or my head should be broken again. I woke up in a ghastly pain and perplexity, but presently fainted once more. When I awoke again to a half-consciousness I felt myself being lifted from the cart and carried, and then flung into the bows of a boat, where I suppose I was joined by the rest of the dismal cart's company.'

It is easy to understand that any man, having escaped the grasp of the press gang, would have little sense of wrong-doing in taking to the life of a smuggler. Loyalty to the law would have died a quick death in the circumstances—if there ever was much of that sentiment in the men of the Ports and Marsh. Most people were involved in the smuggling trade in some way or other, or at any rate in sympathy with it—except the families from whom the customs officers and pre-ventive men were drawn. One cannot help admiring those men who did honestly struggle to enforce the law against such uneven odds. Many were courageous and incorruptible, but others were open to bribes. So the whole business of trying to control so widespread an activity made little impact. How could the smuggler be brought to heel when the very jury, called to give their verdict on a captured smuggler, would never contemplate declaring him guilty? And the magistrates would, as likely as not, have a well-stocked cellar of illicit brandy at home.

From medieval times, therefore, the Marsh and the Cinque Ports were excellent breeding grounds for smugglers. Today many people tend to think of the smuggler of the past as a product of the seventeenth to the early nineteenth centuries—the spirits, tea and tobacco group; but his forerunner was the 'owler', who carried on a moonlit outward traffic, smuggling wool to the Continent. The name originated from his signal, the call of an owl. The later inward contraband consisted of luxuries such as kegs of brandy, tobacco, tea and lace, furtively landed and conveyed (as far as the smugglers of the Cinque Ports and Romney Marsh were concerned) to hiding-places spread thickly through the coastal towns and countryside of Kent and Sussex.

As is always the case in all forms of taxation and customs duties, something that starts on a small scale grows with every crisis and need for national funds; and with increases in tariffs the incentive to smuggle illicit delicacies and luxuries into the country became all the more tempting and worth while. Everyone liked a good cup of tea (far too expensive when obtained by legal means), the tobacco and the brandy which the smuggler provided smoothed the rough corners of life most pleasantly, and how could the farmer's wife and the innkeeper's wife enjoy the luxury of rich lace without the aid of the moonlit trade? It all seemed harmless and reasonable enough—and indeed, as one looks back, it was harmless compared with the activities of present-day smugglers; for what harm did brandy, tobacco, lace and tea do to the nation as a whole when measured against today's smuggled consignments of drugs, which end by ruining young lives?

The 'owlers' were a tougher breed than the brandy, tobacco and tea runners, for wool was for centuries the country's most important and profitable export, and the constant leakage of this valuable national product by illicit means was so serious a loss to the revenue that the death penalty was imposed for outward wool smuggling. This did not, for one moment, stop the trade, but it introduced a more desperate element, and the smugglers became less 'gentlemanly'—readier to eliminate anyone who might inform and lead them to the hangman's rope. To the secrecy of the wool smugglers, and the natural cooperation of the sheep farmers, fear was introduced among the community, for anyone suspected of disloyalty to the 'owling' fraternity could be quickly disposed of.

There was not much danger of disloyalty, however, in the Cinque Ports area and in the Marsh in particular, for in this respect sympathy was with the lawless and most people enjoyed the benefits. Only in the case of two especially ruthless groups —the eighteenth-century Hawkhurst Gang, and the nineteenth-century Aldington Gang—was general animosity aroused, for these were not the gentlemen of the trade but ruffians heartily loathed by all. When the Hawkhurst Gang patronized the inns of the Sussex–Kent border country (which was their special territory) no one dared to interfere with them, and William Holloway, the historian of Rye, described how the Hawkhurst smugglers were seen, after completing a successful run, refreshing themselves in the bar of Rye's Mermaid Inn, 'carousing and smoking their pipes with their loaded pistols on the table before them, no magistrate daring to interfere with them'.

Eventually the Hawkhurst Gang went too far and thereby produced one of the rare occasions in smuggling history when the people of the countryside turned against them. This opposition took concrete form at Goudhurst, one of the most picturesque of Kentish villages, with magnificent views from its churchyard over the Weald. The leading spirit was a man named Sturt, who enrolled recruits and drilled a band of militia so effectively that when the Hawkhurst Gang descended on the village they were routed. Goudhurst was never troubled by them again, and in the end the whole area was freed of their visitations, for the leaders were caught and hanged and thereafter the power of the gang was broken.

The Aldington Gang of a century later were equally tough and ruthless, and these unlikeable characters were often to be seen in the inns of Aldington and Bonnington, the two villages—so peaceful today—which are described in the chapter on the clifftop road.

This gang figured in the 'Battle of Brookland' of 1821, one of the fiercest battles recorded between the smugglers of the Marsh and the preventive men.

The 'owlers' were still in operation but tending to decline when Daniel Defoe wrote his *Tour through the Whole Island of Great Britain* (published 1724–26), and this is how he describes encountering a group of preventive men along the Romney Marsh shore:

'As I rode along this coast, I perceiv'd several dragoons, riding officers, and others arm'd and on horseback, riding always about as if they were huntsmen beating up their game; upon inquiry I found their diligence was employ'd in quest of the owlers, as they call them, and sometimes they catch some of them; but when I came to enquire farther, I found too, that often times these are attack'd in the night, with such numbers, that they dare not resist, or if they do, they are wounded and beaten and sometimes kill'd; and at other times are oblig'd, as it were, to stand still, and see the wool carry'd off before their faces, not daring to meddle; and the boats taking it in from the very horses backs, go immediately off, and are on the coast of France, before any notice can be given of them, while the other are as nimble to return with their horses to their haunts and retreats, where they are not easily found out. But I find so many of these desperate fellows are of late taken up, by the courage and vigilence of the soldiers, that the knots are very much broken, and the owling-trade much abated, at least on that side; the French also finding means to be supply'd from Ireland with much less hazard, and at very little more expence.'

Hastings, Winchelsea and Rye, Dover and Deal, Folkestone, Hythe and Lympne, Dymchurch, Lydd and Dungeness—all were hotbeds of smuggling, and there is little wonder that John Wesley found it an uphill task when he tried, in the eighteenth century, to woo the people of these parts from their smuggling habits. He even published a pamphlet entitled *A Word to a Smuggler* in an effort to get his message across, and he implored them to give up 'the accursed thing, smuggling'. They listened to him with due attention and deference—and probably landed a cargo that very night.

All along the Cinque Ports coastline and throughout the Marsh the traces of the 'gentlemen' are to be found. Only as recently as the 1960's a hiding-place full of contraband kegs came to light during repairs to the south wall of the Hastings Arms tavern in George Street, Hastings. There, in a recess beneath a first-floor window, several great barrels were discovered; the brewers kept one, the Hastings Museum another, and one still remains in position in the Hastings Arms. The Stag Inn in All Saints Street, Hastings, has a notable smugglers' tunnel which led from the inn's underground vault to a cave half-way up the cliffside (the Stag Inn is mentioned more fully in my chapter on Hastings).

In the Flushing Inn at Rye there is an underground vault of great antiquity which is known to have been used by the smugglers to good advantage; but the whole of Rye was riddled with the smuggling fraternity and their accomplices—despite the fact that there was a customs service established in their very midst. The most important families of Rye, the Lambs and the Jeakes, were both connected with the customs service. When I went into the little bakery in Market Street, opposite the Flushing Inn, to see their 200-years'-old brick oven in which the delicious bread for the Flushing Inn is baked, I discovered that this old building, too, had its hiding-place for contraband. The bakehouse chimney had a hoist wheel at the top whereby, in the old days, kegs were hauled to the attics. The houses along this side of Market Street are built in one continuous row, and this made it an easy matter to construct a concealed corridor leading through the attics of every house and ending, most conveniently, in a tavern in East Street.

I have told ghost stories already about the ancient castle at Lympne, and to these can be added smugglers' stories too, for the village of Lympne, with its clifftop views over the Marsh, was a great place for the smuggling trade. The cottages, with their windows facing seawards, were excellently suited for signalling to a ship loaded with illicit cargo, and an intriguing tale is told about one of the four-poster beds which now occupies a room in the eastern tower of Lympne Castle, though its smuggling history did not, in fact, take place at Lympne, but at nearby Folkestone.

In the nineteenth century this bed was owned by a Mr. and Mrs. Robinson who lived at the Warren, Folkestone—and Folkestone (Corporate Member of Dover in the Cinque Ports pedigree) was in the thick of the smuggling trade. One dark night there was a great knocking on the door of the Robinsons' house and, when opened by a servant, a band of men forced their way inside. They made their way to the room where Mr. and Mrs. Robinson lay asleep and, wasting no time, woke them and ordered the bewildered couple out of bed; then, lifting the feather mattress, they stowed away beneath it some packages of great weight. The mattress was flung back into position and the peremptory order given, 'No word of this on pain of death'. The strangers then departed, leaving the Robinsons to clamber back into their knobbly bed.

Some hours later the Excisemen arrived, but after a search they went away. Just before dawn the smugglers returned, toppled the luckless Robinsons out of bed once more, and retrieved their contraband; but the combined weight of the packages and the Robinsons had broken the bottom of the bed. 'The bed will be mended and you'll be rewarded' the smugglers announced—for the packages contained gold, and were well worth a goodly reward to them. But Mr. Robinson, by now justifiably out of sorts, retorted that he did not want to be paid for something he had not wanted to do; all he wanted was to be left in peace. So the smugglers went away, doubtless well pleased, and Mr. Robinson paid for the repairs himself. The bed belonged to the Misses Cox of Wye, in Kent, who were the grand-daughters of the Robinsons, and it can be seen today by visitors to Lympne Castle.

Dymchurch has been made famous as a centre of the contraband trade by the fictional Dr. Syn, the parson-smuggler of Russell Thorndike's blood-and-thunder novels of the Marsh, but it is a very different place today from the village he depicted. In fact, so changed is it that when a film was made of the Dr. Syn story Old Romney, instead of Dymchurch, had to be used as the location. However, the Ship Inn at Dymchurch is the one Russell Thorndike was describing in the book, and when I was there in 1971 I noticed on one of the walls of the bar an old smuggler's plan for concealing contraband—a method of floating tubs under water. We can be sure that Dr. Syn and his Sexton, Mr. Mipps, would have needed no tips in this respect. Underwater concealment was frequently used, and it is said that in one manorial pond up to a hundred barrels of contraband spirit could be hidden at a time in a cavern constructed beneath the water.

The dare-devil nature of the smugglers has caught the

imagination of plenty of writers, but no one has conveyed so perfectly as Rudyard Kipling the atmosphere of the laden ponies plodding silently through the dark, their activities known to all, but acknowledged by none when a stranger was around. In his children's book, *Puck of Pook's Hill*, the Smugglers' Song expresses this so superbly that I will quote it in full:

If you wake at midnight, and hear a horse's feet,
Don't go drawing back the blind, or looking in the street,
Them that asks no questions isn't told a lie.
Watch the wall, my darling, while the Gentlemen go by!

> Five-and-twenty ponies,
> Trotting through the dark—
> Brandy for the Parson,
> 'Baccy for the Clerk;
> Laces for a lady; letters for a spy,
And watch the wall, my darling, while the Gentlemen go by!

Running round the woodlump if you chance to find
Little barrels, roped and tarred, all full of brandy-wine;
Don't you shout to come and look, nor take 'em for your play;
Put the brishwood back again—and they'll be gone next day!

If you see the stable-door setting open wide;
If you see a tired horse lying down inside;
If your mother mends a coat cut about and tore;
If the lining's wet and warm—don't you ask no more!

If you meet King George's men, dressed in blue and red,
You be careful what you say, and mindful what is said.
If they call you 'pretty maid' and chuck you 'neath the chin,
Don't you tell where no one is, nor yet where no one's been!

Knocks and footsteps round the house—whistles after dark—
You've no call for running out till the house-dogs bark.
Trusty's here, and Pincher's here, and see how dumb they lie—
They don't fret to follow when the Gentlemen go by!

If you do as you've been told, likely there's a chance
You'll be give a dainty doll, all the way from France,
With a cap of Valenciennes, and a velvet hood—
A present from the Gentlemen, along o' being good!

> Five-and-twenty ponies,
> Trotting through the dark—
> Brandy for the Parson,
> 'Baccy for the Clerk.

Them that asks no questions isn't told a lie—
Watch the wall, my darling, while the Gentlemen go by!

In Kipling's *Dymchurch Flit* (which the Smugglers' Song precedes in *Puck of Pook's Hill*) the closed circle of the people of the Marsh comes before one's eyes. Old Hobden, who lived in the tamed Sussex countryside beyond the Marsh, describes how he wooed a Marsh woman from Dymchurch under the Wall.

'Then she'd be a Pett—or a Whitgift, would she?' asks his companion.

'Whitgift, Hobden answers. 'She growed to be quite reasonable-like after living in the Weald awhile, but our first twenty-year she was odd-fashioned, no bounds . . . She'd read signs, and sinnifications out o' birds flyin', stars fallin', bees hivin', and such. An she'd lie awake listenin' for calls, she said.'

Says his companion, 'That don't prove naught. All Marsh folk has been smugglers since time everlastin'. 'Twould be in her blood to listen out o' nights.'

The churches of the Marsh played their part in the hiding of contraband. Snargate, Brookland, Ivychurch and Fairfield all concealed their quota of illicit kegs in their time. At Ivychurch part of the flooring of the north aisle was removable to enable contraband to be stowed away in the vault beneath, and there is a record of one occasion, at least, when so much brandy and tobacco were stored away in the church that the Sunday morning service had to be cancelled. Parsons, as Kipling implied, often turned a blind eye to such activities, and enjoyed a well-stocked cellar at the vicarage as a result.

26. Landing a cargo of contraband.

In Snargate Church, in the eighteenth and early nineteenth centuries, a section of the north aisle was sealed off by a partition, and this was frequently used as a 'hide' for contraband. On one occasion a substantial haul of illicit tobacco was found in the belfry during a raid by the Excisemen, and a further search revealed a cask of spirit beneath the vestry table. To this church the Rev. Richard Barham of *The Ingoldsby Legends* came as Rector in 1817, an appointment which included the curacy of nearby Warehorne. Of the two villages he chose to live at Warehorne, and this meant frequent journeys home from Snargate late at night. Many a time he met a company of smugglers riding along the lonely and dark lanes of the Marsh, but on recognizing the parson their challenge would change to a greeting, and they always let him

National Maritime Museum, Greenwich.

pass. It is certain that the jovial and warm-hearted author-parson never gave them away.

Squires and parsons, sextons and clerks, farmers and inn-keepers, lords and ladies—all were liable to be on the reception end of the smugglers' game. There was, in fact, little shame in those days in having smugglers in the family, and it is intriguing to realize that the great French Impressionist painter, Alfred Sisley (born in France of English parents, 1839–99) was the grandson of Francis Sisley, a notorious smuggler of the Marsh who lies buried at Lydd. The gentlemen of the trade were usually laid to rest with inscriptions on their tombs that implied a life of total blamelessness, and such is an example at Patcham, near Brighton, commemorating Daniel Scales, a Sussex smuggler of desperate reputation who was shot by an Exciseman in self-defence.

His epitaph reads:

'Sacred to the memory of Daniel Scales, who was unfortunately shot, on Tuesday evening, Nov. 7, 1796.

> Alas! swift flew the fatal lead,
> Which pierced through the young man's head.
> He instant fell, resigned his breath,
> And closed his languid eyes in death.
> And you who to this stone draw near,
> Oh! pray let fall the pitying tear.
> From this sad instance may we all
> Prepare to meet Jehovah's call.'

Another epitaph is to be found in Lydd churchyard on the tomb of George Walker, a smuggler who died aged 36 on 1 August 1819; on being caught by the preventive men he was stabbed to death:

> Let it be known that I am clay,
> A base man took my life away.
> Yet freely do I him forgive
> And hope in heaven we both shall live.
> Wife and children I've left behind,
> And to the Lord I them resign.
> I hope He will their steps attend
> And guide them to a happy end.

Author's note: In this chapter all quotations from *Puck of Pook's Hill* by Rudyard Kipling are reproduced by kind permission of Mrs. George Bambridge and Macmillan & Co. Ltd.

8. New and Old Romney, Lydd and Dymchurch

The Cinque Port of Romney is a small inland town. Once it stood on the wide Bay of Romney, with a prosperous harbour and the coming and going of ships. Here was the mouth of the river Rother, and westwards beside the Rother was the wharf at Old Romney. The gradual deterioration of Old Romney's wharf caused 'New' Romney to come into being, but by the first quarter of the thirteenth century the two Romneys had already acquired their Old and New titles, which indicates just how new New Romney really is. The waters of the bay washed close to the Church of St. Nicholas in those days, and Romney was a place of immense pride and importance.

The Great Storm of 1287 was a disaster from which the Port never recovered. Shingle, mud and silt were flung over the houses and streets with such violence that the mouth of the river was blocked, and the Rother, choked and deprived of its outlet, changed its course. It then flowed to Rye—to that town's great benefit. Without warning, the great days of Romney as a port were over, for, without the river, silting up of the harbour was inevitable. The shore at Littlestone, over a mile away, today shows no heritage of the curve of the Bay of Romney which once sheltered so many ships.

A curiosity of New Romney is that, although on the fringe of the Marsh, it is entirely separate. Its Liberty and jurisdiction are those of a Cinque Port and not of Romney Marsh. In the fourteenth century there was a good deal of friction between the people of the Marsh and the Barons of the Cinque Port of Romney over the artificial watercourse created between Snargate and the sea. This was vital in order to revive the harbour damaged in 1287 and to replace the Rother —but the men of the Marsh deemed this interference in their primary sphere of drainage. On one occasion they even went so far as to destroy the sluice gate built by the Romney

Portsmen at Snargate, thus reducing the harbour to useless-ness. So much trouble developed between Port and Marsh that the King had to intervene.

Up to the fifteenth century efforts were still being made to cut a waterway but it was unavailing—the river had gone, and nothing could be done to win it back or to create a water-way of equal value. So the Portsmen turned from the sea to the land for their livelihood, and New Romney resigned itself to a portless role.

Despite this very early loss of its harbour, Romney has always held a special eminence in the Confederation of the Cinque Ports owing to the fact that it is located almost dead centre between the two groups of the Kent and Sussex Ports. For this reason it was the most suitable place for holding the meetings of the Brodhull and Guestling. And because so many of these meetings were convened here New Romney stored in the Cinque Ports Chest the treasured records of the Confederation, as well as the records of the town itself dating from the fourteenth century. Here, until very recently, were kept the historic White and Black Books of the Cinque Ports— the White Book containing the minutes of the Brodhull from 1433 to 1571 and the Black Book the minutes of the Brodhull and Guestling from 1572. In this chest were pre-served, too, the Bailiff's records of the Yarmouth Herring Fair—the annual event which played so important a part in the lives of the medieval Barons of the Cinque Ports, and which caused so much controversy, squabbling, hatred and brawls.

Just as the Great Storm deprived Romney of its medieval prosperity as a port, so a present-day ruling has divested the town of its status as guardian of the contents of the Cinque Ports Chest. All these records have now been transferred to the County Archives at Maidstone, and it must have been a sad day for New Romney when they were carried away. Perhaps it is for the best that they have gone, however, for these records are irreplaceable and Maidstone is far better equipped for the storage and preservation of such a heritage. A burglary (early in 1971) at the New Romney Town Hall endorses this point, which was also emphasized by the similar burglary at Dover

Museum, resulting in the loss of the historic Silver Oar of the Cinque Ports.

New Romney served a valuable role in past times as mediator when friction developed between the men of the Marsh, the Barons of the Cinque Ports, and the archiepiscopal holders of Church lands in the Marsh. The Portsmen and the Marshmen, as lawless a community as one could find, did not suffer readily any interference with their way of life.

A favourite activity of the people of medieval New Romney was the performance of religious plays. They had their own cycle of mystery plays which bore the collective title of *Le Playbook,* and this, like the more famous York, Chester and Wakefield cycles of mystery plays, introduced plenty of rough humour to the text, which made the scriptures readily understandable to the illiterate in their audiences. In addition to the main performances in New Romney, the players were indefatigable in travelling to remote villages of the Marsh, no mean task with their carts and props in days when the drainage was less efficient than today and the roads appalling.

With the loss of its seafaring life New Romney declined gently over the centuries, but it has succeeded in dwindling with dignity, escaping the onslaught of seaside building which has afflicted its neighbours Dymchurch and St. Mary's Bay.

In New Romney, streets which once existed north of the town gradually disappeared altogether, and of the five churches recorded at the time of the 1086 Domesday survey only St. Nicholas survives—but what a magnificent survival! This church's massive pinnacled tower is a magnet as one approaches from the Marsh, and there is no disappointment in store when it is reached. The Norman tower is majestic and noble, its west doorway sunk so far below ground level that steps lead down to it. This is said to be a heritage of the masses of shingle and mud flung inshore at the time of the Great Storm; inside the church marks can still be seen showing how high the floodwaters of the thirteenth century rose. The fine arches of the Norman nave are wonderfully preserved and the massive piers, alternately octagonal and cylindrical, extend from the pulpit to the western screen. The floor is of ancient,

27. The Church of St. Nicholas, New Romney, whose massive Norman tower is a dramatic landmark as the town is approached from the Marsh.

uneven stones, and the box pews are in perfect harmony with the solid dignity of this splendid church.

St. Nicholas was used from very early times for municipal and Cinque Ports gatherings, and it was around the table tomb of Richard Stuppenye, at the east end of the south aisle, that the Jurats would assemble each year to elect their new Mayor. The inscription on this tomb reads:

'Here lyeth buryed the bodye of Richard Stuppenye Jurate of this towne in the first yeare of K.Hy VIII who dyed in the

78. The sunken west doorway of New Romney's Church of St. Nicholas is believed to be due to the vast amount of shingle and mud which piled up against the church during the Great Storm of 1287. The thirteenth-century floodwater marks are still visible inside the church.

XVIII yeare of the sayde kynges reigne of whose memorye Clement Stuppenye of the same port his great grandsonne hath caused this tombe to be new erected for the use of the ancient meeting and election of maior and jurats of this port towne.'

These elections beside the Stuppenye tomb date back to the beginning of the Port's mayoral status, for here was elected the first Mayor of New Romney during the reign of Queen Elizabeth I. The practice continued until a nineteenth-century Act of Parliament barred the use of churches for such municipal purposes. There had long been unrest in some circles over the custom, and in the fifteenth century the vicar put forward a request that the Jurats should not hold their session in his church at the same time as Divine Service was being celebrated. However, the holding of such meetings in parish churches was a general practice, and in Dover it was not only the Mayor and Members of Parliament who were elected within the sacred walls of St. Mary-the-Virgin, but the Mayor and Corporation sat smugly in box pews *behind* the altar during religious services. King Charles II was so incensed at the sight of them when he attended Divine Service at Dover in 1670 that he ordered the box pews of the Mayor and Corporation to be nailed up! Such misuse of churches obviously had to be curtailed, and eventually it was; but nevertheless one would like to think of the Jurats of New Romney still assembling in all their dignity around the tomb of Richard Stuppenye to elect their new Mayor.

There used to be an interesting little museum in the Town Hall at New Romney where all sorts of exhibits helped to provide the background of this much-diminished Cinque Port. The exhibits included ancient coins from the town's own mint. But when I called there early in 1971 the burglary —which I have already mentioned—had just taken place and the remains of the museum exhibits were scattered in turmoil. At the time there was doubt whether it would ever be opened again, but now I understand that the showcase is being reorganized. The 'Brasen Horne of Saylence', whose notes used to announce the opening of the Yarmouth Herring Fair, still hangs on the wall of the council chamber, and New Romney still possesses its section of the canopy borne at the coronation of King George III. But the ancient coins, which were the special treasure of the museum, are gone.

Old Romney, two and a half miles to the west, is one of the most tranquil of all the villages of this Cinque Port and Marsh countryside, and here it is even more impossible than at New Romney to believe in the seafaring activities of the wharf of long ago. Although only a very short distance from the New Romney to Brenzett road, it seems miles from anywhere. There is something softer and gentler about Old Romney than

29. The font in St. Clement's Church, Old Romney. This dates from about 1300 and is of exceptional interest for the rarity of the carved capitals, each different, of the circular supports.

any of the other villages of the area—a 'something' difficult to describe but immediately sensed. Sheep graze up to the very doors of the old church, but this is not the wide, dyke-intersected pasturage typical of the Marsh, for close to the church is an orchard, with all the light and shade beneath the branches which an orchard brings. The few houses are

E

built in a mellower Georgian mould than those of the remoter hamlets.

The church at Old Romney is dedicated to St. Clement, and in this Cinque Port area of receding seas there could surely be no more appropriate saint. Traditionally St. Clement suffered martyrdom by drowning in the sea with an anchor fixed around his neck, and legend also relates that afterwards the ocean miraculously receded three miles, revealing the saint's body in a stone chest, with the anchor by his side. For some time afterwards, so the legend tells, the sea repeated its recession annually on the day of his martyrdom, leaving the land dry for the following six days.

St. Clement's Church must, long ago, have stood near the wharf when the whole area was alive with ships and seamen, for it dates back to very early days. The nave was constructed during the first century of the Norman Conquest, and the north and south aisles were added in about 1200. Continual additions have, in fact, been made to this small church, and whereas this can sometimes be disturbing, in St. Clement's it seems merely a reflection of long continuity of worship. There is a charm and naturalness about the mixture of periods —for instance, at the west end, where an eighteenth-century minstrel's gallery with slender supporting columns contrasts strikingly with the massive and ancient roof beams above. In the north chapel is a stone coffin of great antiquity.

The tomb of a former Huguenot rector occupies the centre of the chancel floor. This commemorates John Deffray, one of the many Protestants who sought refuge along this Cinque Port shore from religious persecution in France. Like so many of the Huguenot and Flemish refugees, he contributed greatly to the well-being of the country of his adoption, and was a respected rector of the parish of Old Romney from 1690 until his death. His tombstone records that 'After Delight in doing Good He departed this life Sept: ye 4th 1738 in ye 78th Year of His Age'. He was rector of St. Clement's for almost half a century.

The font, dating from about 1300, is very unusual. The bowl set in a solid square block of stone is plain enough; but it is supported on four circular shafts, each with a different, though much worn, carved capital. Miss Anne Roper, in her marvellously informative church guide, helps to identify these carvings, and points out that 30 years ago, when she first wrote the guide, they were much clearer than they are today. She records that the tiny figures on the capitals represent a little dwarfish man with hands on knees, another with fingers in mouth, a third with a monkey's face, and the fourth a priest. It is sad that these figures have so nearly weathered away—but far, far better than that they should have acquired the polished nothingness of restoration. The means of reaching the church bells is one of those rough ladder-stairways made from hewn tree-trunks which are, very occasionally, encountered in the towers of ancient churches. There is another at Hever, also in Kent, in the church where Anne Boleyn worshipped in her girlhood days—the days before Henry VIII, a queen's crown, and the executioner followed in quick succession.

Lydd, Romney's Corporate Member, seems wider awake today than its Head Port, for the town lies on the road to the nuclear power station at Dungeness, and Ferryfield airport is only three-quarters of a mile from the centre of Lydd. The shingle territory of Dungeness lies within the Borough of Lydd.

By the ninth century both Romney and Lydd already possessed harbours, but whereas Romney lay within the sheltering arm of Romney Bay, Lydd was, in those early days, an island. Midley, now represented only by a lonely ruined arch (all that remains of its church) was also at that time an island lying between Lydd and Romney.

There has, in the past, been something of the character of a frontier town about Lydd—with its reputation for old-time smuggling and the establishment, towards the end of the last century, of a military camp with artillery ranges; in fact, it was at Lydd, in 1888, that the explosive 'lyddite' was first tested, so gaining its name. But despite lyddite, rifle ranges, the nearby nuclear power station and the airport, there is a surprisingly tranquil appeal about Lydd, especially in the area around its fine church. To gain this impression of calm, however, it is necessary to come to the town from the Marsh—by the turning from the Brookland to Rye road, which leads past the Woolpack Inn. This road follows a rural marshland route all the way until it suddenly ends in the very centre of Lydd, opposite the church.

The Parish Church of All Saints is the glory of Lydd, and the severe damage which it suffered from enemy action was one of the architectural tragedies of the last war. A bomb fell in 1940 and completely destroyed the chancel; then, in 1944, further damage resulted during the flying-bomb attacks. The healing of the church, with all its former grandeur revived, has been a triumph of local determination and pride—and how successful this restoration has been! Here is sensed none of the regret left by Victorian restoration, for the beauty has been superbly retained.

The church is of stately proportions, 199 feet in length with a tower rising to 132 feet. The height of the tower dates from the early sixteenth century when it was raised by Thomas Wolsey (later Cardinal Wolsey), then Rector of Lydd. Of greatest antiquity is the Baptistry where the massive unplastered walls of stone are the remains of the Saxon church from which All Saints has grown. The plain, uncluttered dignity of these Saxon walls is unforgettably impressive.

There are a couple of tombs of special interest in the North Chapel. One bears the medieval effigy of a Crusader, and this is attributed to Sir Walter de Menyl of Lydd. The other is the tomb of Clement Stuppenye, the 'great grandsonne' of Richard Stuppenye of New Romney, around whose tomb in the Church of St. Nicholas the Jurats gathered to elect their Mayor. The tomb of Clement Stuppenye served a similar purpose at Lydd, for around it would assemble the Commonalty for the election of the Jurats. Lydd did not have a Mayor until 1885 when (as in Hythe, recorded on John Bredgman's tomb) the last Bailiff was also the first Mayor.

The chancel is, owing to its predecessor's total wartime destruction, completely new and very beautiful. Its ceiling is ornamented with coloured bosses of oak leaf and Tudor Rose design, and the austere but elegant modern altar rails of stainless steel contrast in their plainness but combine most excellently. I have not seen a more successful restoration than this. Among numerous monumental brasses in the church the earliest commemorates John Thomas of c. 1429.

Epitaph enthusiasts will find a good one for their collection in Lydd churchyard. This commemorates Tom Edgar, who sailed as first mate with Captain James Cook on the fatal voyage which ended with the death of Captain Cook in 1779 at the hands of the natives of Hawaii. Tom Edgar was with him, and saw him stabbed and clubbed to death on the seashore; he gave evidence at the subsequent inquiry. Edgar rose to be a lieutenant in the Royal Navy, but it is said that further advancement was handicapped by his liking for grog! The epitaph reads:

> Tom Edgar at last has sailed out of this world,
> His shroud is put on, his topsails are furl'd.
> He lies snug in death's boat, without any concern
> And is moored for a full due ahead and astern.
> O'er the Compass of Life he has merrily run,
> His voyage is completed, his reckoning is done.

Dymchurch is another place which has played an important part in the affairs of the Marsh in the past, but today its Marshland character is obscured. It has become a highly popular seaside resort, and obviously gives pleasure to enormous numbers of people in this role—which comprises holiday chalets, bungalows, caravans, cafés and gift shops, together with a fun fair. The shade of Dr. Syn is constantly evoked, despite the fact that the Dymchurch of today bears little resemblance to the old smugglers' Dymchurch which was the scene of Russell Thorndike's *Dr. Syn* novels.

Having made these sombre remarks, however, I will continue by saying that there is some worthwhile exploration to be done in Dymchurch. The three-miles-long Dymchurch Wall is, in itself, of extreme interest, for it is the modern successor of previous earthworks and barriers which have been holding back the sea for centuries. Without the wall, and its system of sluices, Romney Marsh would not exist.

One of the peculiarities of Dymchurch, as a result, is that it must be one of the few stretches of coastline where the owners of sea-front bungalows have absolutely no view of the sea at all. They look out on to the great ledge of the Dymchurch Wall, with its Martello Towers occasionally breaking the symmetry of its outline, and they must climb steps to the top of the wall and down the other side in order to reach the beach. The sight of the wall must be comforting all the same, for the history of the sea's cruelty in these parts makes this great barrier a friend rather than an enemy.

The New Hall in Dymchurch is of special interest—a building which, like New Romney, was only new long ago. It dates from 1580, when it replaced an earlier half-timbered building destroyed by fire. Dymchurch was the seat of government of the Marsh, and here, in the New Hall, met the Lords of the Level—the Lords, Bailiff and Jurats of Romney Marsh—to discuss and rule the marshland which was their domain. It was the efficient maintenance of the walls and drainage of the Marsh which was their primary concern, vital to the very existence of the Marsh and its people; for this reason they had unique rights which enabled them to enforce upkeep and finance. The Grand Lath of the Lords, Bailiff and Jurats of Romney Marsh is still held annually at Dymchurch, but legislation has swept away their ruling powers.

In the New Hall there is a perfect and unspoilt example of an old Court Room, and this is now used as a small museum. Here will be found a printed version of Henry iii's Charter relating to Romney Marsh, which reads: 'To all his Bailiffs and faithful Subjects to whom these Letters shall come, Greeting; Because by four and twenty lawful Men of Rumney Marsh (Time out of Mind) thereunto chosen and sworn, Distresses ought to be made upon all those which have Lands and Tenements in the said Marsh, to repair the Walls and Watergages of the same against the Dangers of the Sea . . .' Here too, is an extract from a document held in Lambeth Palace in London, which dates from the reign of Queen Mary i: 'Expenditor—Ye shall well and truly endeavour yourself upon making and repayring and amending of the see walles belonygne to Romeney Marshe both at Dymchurch and Apuldore for withal knockes, relayes, slattes, groynes, fotehegges and other necessaires for defence of the said walles or any of them heretofore advysed and assygned to be don, ye shall do in likewys to the gutts of Sherlock and the watergangs of the same, Willop Wall and the Grene Walls.' Well, no doubt the meaning was absolutely clear; we can only hope that there was no misunderstanding over Sherlock's gutts.

There are a couple of printed copies of the Charter of Romney Marsh, one of 1597 and the other of 1647; and also, among many other items, a fifteenth-century seal of the Bailiff of Romney Marsh, with a couple of sixteenth and seventeenth-century seals of the Corporation of Romney Marsh.

The Court Room still has its Upper Chair where the Magistrate would sit when the courts were held here (up to 1951, the year when the final court was held). In this old Court Room it is easy to visualize the *Dr. Syn* inquiry into the murder of Sennacherib Pepper, the Dymchurch doctor of the tale. This is, too, the Court Room of the story, *Jerry Jarvis's Wig*, in *The Ingoldsby Legends*.

The Church of St. Peter and St. Paul at Dymchurch was built in the twelfth century but has been much altered and restored since. A picture which shows it before alteration in 1821 depicts a most individual and charming little church— and it is very charming still, though not so unusual. It was the increase in population which caused the church to be enlarged, and in so doing the Norman north wall was demolished and the old steepled tower, similar to the one at Old Romney, was removed. It is for this reason that Old Romney was so appropriate a place to be used for the filming of *Dr. Syn* in the 1960's. Apart from the north wall, the original Norman walls of the church remain, as do the Norman south and west doorways (the latter now on the inside wall of the Tower). In the churchyard are a number of tombstones with skull and crossbone ornamentation—a reflection of eighteenth-century taste in tombstones and having no connection with the well-known addiction to piracy as well as smuggling along this shore in the old days.

The Ship Inn is, of course, the real headquarters of Dr. Syn's fictional existence, and the inn keeps up the smuggling theme with enthusiasm. There are various framed items of

30. 'Jerry Jarvis's Wig', one of the Reverend Richard H. Barham's *Ingoldsby Legends*, had the Court Room of Dymchurch's New Hall as the setting for the murder trial. This illustration to the story was by George Cruikshank. The Dymchurch Court Room also figures in Russell Thorndike's *Dr. Syn*.

smuggling interest on the walls, including the record of a Dymchurch gang of smugglers who, in 1787, exported to France a boatload of live sheep—for the value of meat as well as wool! The gang were caught, tried at the New Hall, and committed to the adjoining jail. They escaped with the aid of friends at the Ship Inn—almost a foregone conclusion in this area where everyone was on the side of the smuggler.

There is no question of seeing the last of Dr. Syn in Dymchurch, and at the time of writing he and his smuggler friends have just been brought to life in a big way, with the whole Dymchurch community in carnival mood for a 'Day of Syn'! Russell Thorndike's slippery parson–smuggler has, indeed, taken over 'Dymchurch under the Wall'.

9. Other Churches of the Marsh

One of the phenomenal aspects of the Marsh is its churches—not just an odd small church or chapel here and there among the scattered population, but great, lonely churches of distinction. Most of them are quite different in character, yet have common Marshland features; and one of these is the round or oval painted text boards perched high on pillars or arches, pronouncing words of wisdom to the congregation below. Sometimes these text boards are plain, sometimes they have an ornamental border; all had their origin in the days of the Reformation.

Imposing versions of the royal coat of arms are found in many of these churches. Royal portraits in sculptured form were frequently incorporated in medieval church ornamentation (such as, for instance, the heads of Edward I and Edward II in the Alard Chantry at Winchelsea); after the Reformation, however, which brought removal or defacement of so many of the sculptured images, a decorative painted version of the royal arms became an ornamental substitute. This was in recognition of the monarch's new role as head of the Church in place of Papal supremacy. With the Cromwellian victory in the Civil War of the seventeenth century, down came the royal arms; but with the restoration of the monarchy in 1660, up they went again. Most of the existing royal arms in the Marshland churches date from Georgian times.

The size of these lonely churches is so surprising that William Cobbett, in his *Rural Rides* of the 1820's, explodes with indignation, his target this time being 'the vagabonds'—who are seemingly the same as 'the Thing' of his Martello Tower outburst. The chip on his shoulder is weighing heavily by the time he reaches the sea near New Romney. He writes as follows:

'At three miles from Appledore I came through Snargate, a

village with five houses, and with a church capable of containing two thousand people! The vagabonds tell us, however, that we have a wonderful increase of population! . . .
At Brenzett (a mile farther on) I with great difficulty got a
rasher of bacon for breakfast. The few houses that there are
are miserable in the extreme. The church here (only a mile
from the last) nearly as large; and nobody to go to it. What!
Will the vagabonds attempt to make us believe that these
churches were built for nothing!'

He then goes on to describe, in more cheerful vein, the
phenomenal fertility of the soil at Old Romney, but continues:

'At this Old Romney there is a church (two miles only from
the last, mind!) fit to contain one thousand five hundred
people, and there are for the people of the parish to live
in twenty-two or twenty-three houses! and yet the vagabonds have the impudence to tell us, that the population of
England has vastly increased . . .'

It is fortunate that Cobbett missed the lane which leads from
Brenzett to Ivychurch, for here (only a short distance from
the churches at Brenzett, Snargate, Old and New Romney)
is another church of such massive proportions, among its
small cluster of houses, that the sight of it would have made
him fume with rage. For the rest of us, who do not share
Cobbett's inflammable susceptibilities, these churches are a
superb heritage. We have to remember, however, that great
hardship was suffered by farm labourers at the time of his
Rides, as instanced by the story of Sir William Cosway at
Bilsington, who lent £150 in 1830 to the villagers to enable
families to emigrate to America. There was also the habit of
some less responsible Rectors in accepting livings and re-
maining practically unknown to the parishioners. But the
people of the Marsh never did welcome strangers gladly, and I
suspect that Cobbett's poor reception at Brenzett was due to
his untimely arrival—just as the latest hoard of contraband
spirit was being stowed away through a trap door in the
floor!
    I will start my description of these Marshland churches with

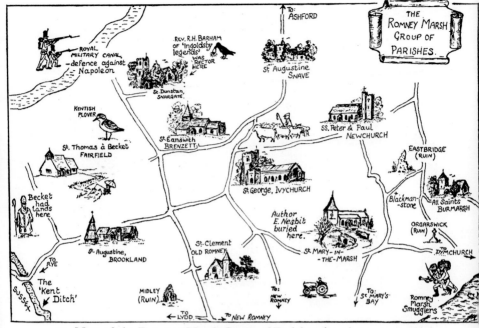

Map of the Romney Marsh Group of Parishes

TO: ASHFORD

THE ROMNEY MARSH GROUP OF PARISHES.

ROYAL MILITARY CANAL —defence against Napoleon

REV. R.H. BARHAM or 'Ingoldsby' legends' WAS RECTOR HERE

St. Dunstan, SNARGATE

St. Augustine SNAVE

KENTISH PLOVER

St. Eanswith BRENZETT

SS. Peter & Paul NEWCHURCH

EASTBRIDGE (RUIN)

St. Thomas à Becket FAIRFIELD

St. George, IVYCHURCH

Blackman-stone

All Saints BURMARSH

Becket had lands here

Author E. Nesbit buried here.

ORGARSWICK (RUIN)

TO RYE

St. Augustine, BROOKLAND

St. Clement OLD ROMNEY

St. Mary-in-the-Marsh

DYMCHURCH

The 'Kent Ditch'

MIDLEY (RUIN)

TO: NEW ROMNEY

TO: St. MARY'S BAY

Romney Marsh Smugglers

SUSSEX

TO LYDD

TO NEW ROMNEY

31. Map of the Romney Marsh Group of Parishes, by whose courtesy it is reproduced.

St. George's at Ivychurch—the church that Cobbett missed. It dates from the fourteenth century and is vast and impressive, with a great square tower and a south porch which, embattled and buttressed, seems to be competing with the tower for size.

St. George's has, in its time, suffered severe damage and neglect. During the Civil War Cromwell's soldiers slept within its walls and stabled their horses there. And Ivychurch seems, in past days, to have had more than its share of invisible Rectors. In the nineteenth century, for instance, there was George Robert Gleig, Rector from 1822 to 1880, but since he was also Chaplain General to the Forces from 1846 to 1875 and held various other appointments, he rarely appeared at Ivychurch at all. It was during this Rector's incumbency that the Archbishop came to the village and, on inquiring about the Rector, was told that no one had seen him for 40 years. The diplomatic Archbishop is said to have replied that they would find him most agreeable when they met him!

32. St. George's Church, Ivychurch. This massive and very fine fourteenth-century church dominates the small village in which it stands. Its buttressed south porch is also of massive proportions.

Among the records at Ivychurch is a churchwardens' complaint that the Rector 'has never come among us sith his induction . . . the parish church is sorely decayed, and likely to fall down'.

Happily this splendid church did not fall down, and the solidity of its appearance implies that it will not easily do so. But at the end of the nineteenth century it was in a deplorable state. Miss Anne Roper, who has written the very informative church guide, tells us how at this time every window was broken, the roof open to the sky in many places, and the church a tragic picture of desolation, occupied by bats, mice and the decaying bodies of dead owls. The Rector who inherited this problem in 1903 achieved miracles of transformation, but further damage was inflicted when the tower was struck by lightning. When I visited Ivychurch in 1970 there was still a sadly barren air within the church; but when I

opened the door in May 1971 there was a miraculous change.
Restoration is now being undertaken by the Friends of Kent
Churches and St. George's is coming to life in marvellous
fashion.

The church is broad, bare and very light owing to its
possession of a clerestory. The royal coat of arms is of the
reign of George III, 1775, and there are some good examples
of the Marshland text boards. A curiosity in the south aisle is a
'Hudd', a kind of sentry-box to be carried to the graveside for
protection of the Minister during rainy burials. The north
aisle has served several purposes in addition to its main role—
as the village school towards the end of the nineteenth
century and, at an earlier date, as a hiding-place for smugglers'

33. **Brookland's detached belfry**
is a famous and very curious
feature of the Church of St.
Augustine.

contraband, when some of its flooring would be removed to
give access to the vault below. Miss Roper relates an amusing
incident of the old smuggling days—an occasion when the
Sunday service had to be cancelled altogether owing to the
glut of contraband occupying the church; but for the full
story of this the church guide must be bought.

It is not far from Ivychurch to the thirteenth-century Church of St. Augustine at Brookland—possibly the best known of all the Marshland churches. Brookland Church is not, in fact, remote like some of the others, for it is on the busy New Romney to Rye road. Its fame has grown, not only for the quality of the church itself, but for the curiosity of its detached wooden bell-tower, which stands between the road and the church with the mixed air of a pagoda and a massively proportioned candle-snuffer.

The tales about Brookland's detached belfry are many, the most usual being that the morals of the Marsh were so slack in past days that the shock of a couple coming to the church to be married was too much for the belfry, which toppled over in amazement. Another anecdote is that the belfry was twice erected in its proper position, and twice came down in gales, so in the end remained earthbound. A third story tells of the master mason who set out the plans for the

34. The |Norman |lead font in Brookland Church is of outstanding interest. In a perfect state of preservation, it dates from 1150 and is completely covered with ornamentation.

church on two pieces of parchment, the steeple on one and the body of the church on the other—and the builders carried this out to the letter. The real reason seems to be that owing to the marshy soil in which the foundations stand it was felt safer to have a detached belfry—and the wisdom of this is seen by the outward leaning aspect of the nave arches.

The church is of majestic proportions, and has the element

of bare austerity often encountered in churches of the Marsh; but it is soon evident that in addition to its curious bell tower there are many reasons why this church is so remarkable. Its Norman lead font, in particular, is considered to be the most important of its kind in the country and, dated 1150, is older than the church itself. The ornamentation covers every inch of it, and being of lead is as clear today as when twelfth-century hands completed it. At the top are two lines of cable design and one line of tooth pattern; the arcades below are sculptured with the signs of the Zodiac; and lower still are the Occupations of the Months, taken from the calendars of early psalters. The months are named in Norman French characters of the twelfth century.

In the south-west corner of the church is a rural screen known as a Tithe Pen, complete with its set of weights, scales and measures; by the vestry door is a large chest which is believed to have come from a Spanish galleon at the time of the Armada. The fifteenth-century benches were made from the timber of the old rood screen, and the high pews are Georgian.

At the east end of the south aisle is the remainder of a medieval wall painting depicting the assassination of St. Thomas Becket—very dim, but the subject is quite clearly recognizable. This painting was uncovered in 1964.

It is not very far from Brookland to Fairfield Church, although the route is difficult to find unless you are quite clear that you must follow the road to Appledore and Tenterden. Then suddenly this isolated little church is seen in pasture-land to the right of the road, sheep grazing up to its door and its outline reflected in a neighbouring dyke. In times of flood this church used literally to sail in a marshland lake, but improved drainage has prevented this in recent years. The mounting block used by parishioners arriving on horseback still stands outside. This charming little church is of fourteenth-century construction but was much rebuilt in the eighteenth century and very ably restored in 1913.

Most people are mystified to find Fairfield Church in so isolated a spot, without even a cottage to keep it company, and, like Brookland's bell-tower, this has given rise to stories

concerning its origin. One is this: an Archbishop of Canterbury, or high church dignitary, was on his way across the
Marsh when (like many a later traveller, and certainly like
the excisemen who attempted to chase smugglers across the
Marsh by night) he fell into an unseen dyke. With his heavy
clothing he sank quickly, and was just surfacing for the third
time when a farmer saw him and fished him out. In thanksgiving he erected the church and dedicated it to St. Thomas
Becket. Another version of this tale says that as the church
dignitary rose for the first time he prayed 'St. Thomas, save
me!'; but he sank. On rising for the second time his words
were more urgent. 'St. Thomas, save me and I will build a
church to your glory' was his plea. He rose for the third time—
and there was the farmer who hauled him out. So he built the
church and dedicated it to St. Thomas Becket in fulfilment of
his vow. And the farmer? No tale relates that he received
anything at all.

St. Dunstan's at Snargate stands sheltered by trees and is
especially notable as having been the church where the author
of *The Ingoldsby Legends* was incumbent. The Reverend Richard
Harris Barham became Rector in 1817, as a young man of 28
years, and the appointment at Snargate was combined with the
curacy at Warehorne, where he lived.

Two years after coming to Snargate Barham suffered a
broken leg when the gig in which he was travelling overturned; but misfortune became good fortune, for it was the
inactivity caused by the accident that set his pen running. The
success of his verse-legends was immense during his lifetime,
although the style is too rollicking and jingling for present-day
tastes. Had he kept to his prose stories—such as *Mrs. Botherby's
Story*, in which he displays a slightly Trollopian (though more
verbose) turn of humour, he would probably still be read today.

At Snargate, therefore, we can imagine Richard Harris
Barham first taking up his literary pen, and it was in fact prose
that he adopted as his media at this time—a novel entitled
Baldwin which seemingly enjoyed no success at all. It was
followed by *My Cousin Nicholas*, another novel which was still
incomplete when he left Snargate to move to London, where

35. St. Dunstan's Church, Snargate, to which the future author of the *Ingoldsby Legends*, the Rev. Richard H. Barham, came as Rector in 1817. This church was at one time a favourite hiding-place for smugglers' contraband.

he had been elected a minor canon of St. Paul's Cathedral. So his 'Legends' never emanated from Snargate, but his first literary inspiration did.

In this whole area of the Marsh and the Cinque Ports the story of St. Thomas Becket constantly arises, and at Snargate, with the name of Richard Harris Barham, it rises once more—but in unusual form; for Barham, surprisingly, took great pride in claiming descent from one of the four assassins,

Reginald FitzUrse. He maintained that this inglorious ancestor fled from Canterbury to Ireland, and there assumed the name MacMahon which, according to Barham, held the same meaning, in the ancient Irish tongue, as his own FitzUrse title. FitzUrse, or rather MacMahon, then headed for Rome, to seek dispensation from the Pope, and ended his wanderings in the Holy Land, where he died. His brother, Robert, inherited the family estates, and following the MacMahon principle of concealing the name on which so heavy a cloud now lay, he became De Berham, still retaining the original meaning of the name FitzUrse. Eventually this became simplified to Barham. That, at any rate, is the theory of the author of *The Ingoldsby Legends*.

The name Snargate owes its derivation to a 'snare-gate' or sluice-gate erected here in 1254 to aid in the maintenance of the waterway which flowed from Appledore to Romney. In 1821, when Cobbett rode by, there were 15 dwellings in the parish—of which only five caught the irate eye of the rural rider.

The Church of St. Dunstan at Snargate probably looks much the same externally as it did in the Reverend Richard Barham's day, but how much finer it would have been if the interior had not been 'improved upon' by a well-meaning restoration in the 1870's. As in many of the Marshland churches, there is no chancel arch in St. Dunstan's. An important new discovery at the time of writing is a wall painting, the Tudor Great Ship (dated 1480–1520), now visible on the north wall. At the eastern end of the north aisle is the section which was once walled off and formed so admirable a hiding-place for the Marshland smugglers' contraband. The roof of this north aisle is especially interesting, for at the centre of five of the fourteenth-century tie beams are bosses which portray fourteenth-century landowners of the parish.

At Newchurch is the very fine Church of St. Peter and St. Paul, built in the thirteenth century but enlarged in the fourteenth, with a sturdy buttressed tower of late fourteenth or early fifteenth-century date. It is a beautiful church, with something of the sturdiness and majesty of Ivychurch but none of its sense of bareness and past tribulations. The tower, although of

such great solidity, leans to the west, and the stone doorway in
the north wall of the tower has also sunk to a sideways angle.

The Tudor Rose is prominent in the decoration, and is to
be found in the wooden roof bosses of the chancel, as well as on
the font; but what is especially unusual on the font shields is
the combination of both the White Rose of York and the Red
Rose of Lancaster, as well as the Tudor Rose. It is suggested
that this may have symbolized thanksgiving for the end of the
Wars of the Roses, with all the disruption and torn loyalties
which they brought in their wake.

The South Chapel is entered by a fifteenth-century oak
screen, which is thought to have been made from the rood
screen. In the North Chapel the ancient carved vestment chest
now forms the altar, and in this chapel there are some interesting relics of the early ornamentation of the church—fragments of stained glass and stonework, and also a startling

36. Carved wooden head at Newchurch. This strange face was removed from the roof of the Church
of St. Peter and St. Paul during
restoration in the early part of this
century. It is now preserved in the
South Chapel together with other
examples of the early ornamentation
of the church.

head of carved wood which was removed from the roof
during the restoration of 1909–1915.

The expression of this face is curious to say the least, and
between the teeth is grasped something round and large, like
a ball or stone. This is usually described as the tongue lolling
out, but if the tongue had swelled up to this state of solid

roundness it would well explain the expression of horror on the face. Personally, I am not convinced that it is a tongue, although I am assured by much sounder authorities than myself that this is so; to me, it looks like a gag against gossip and lies. Whatever is grasped so fiercely between this man's teeth has been there a very long time, and from his expression he is heartily tired of it.

These are my favourite churches of the Marsh. There are others to visit: at St. Mary-in-the-Marsh, where the writer E. Nesbit lies buried; at Burmarsh, where so much of the pasture-land has gone over to cultivation that the true Marshland character is lost; Snave, hidden in trees; Warehorne, where 'Tom Ingoldsby' lived—this was the pseudonym under which Barham wrote his *Legends*; Brenzett, which earned such scorn from Cobbett; and the strange, barn-like church in a meadow at East Guldeford.

Appledore is not strictly of the Marsh at all, for it is located on the far bank of the Royal Military Canal, which forms the northern boundary of Romney Marsh. Already a change of character seems to have taken place when one crosses the bridge over the Canal and walks into Appledore, for here the spacious street seems to have more in common with Tenterden than with the villages of the Marsh. The Church of St. Peter and St. Paul stands as neighbour to the village inn, and there is a comfortable air about everything.

The land on the southern side of the Canal is, however, the lowest area of the Marsh, and therefore it has suffered more flooding in the past than anywhere else. It is lower than the area by the Dymchurch Wall, and for this reason upkeep of two barriers, the Great Wall and Little Wall of Appledore (or Apuldre, as it is called in early writings) was of the greatest urgency in days gone by. Today modern drainage, and the Royal Military Canal into which flood-water is pumped, have come to the rescue of this low-lying part of the Marsh.

The lonely and very beautiful Marshland churches have, since 1962, been gathered together to form part of the Romney Marsh Group of Parishes. They are cared for and loved, and the Rector of the Group, whose vicarage is at Ivychurch, is far removed from the 'invisible' Rectors who once figured in

Ivychurch's history. With the aid of two assistant priests, services are held in the individual churches, and there is also a monthly group service, for which parishioners are collected by the Group of Parishes mini-bus or a coach.

Even Cobbett, were he to embark upon another of his *Rural Rides* today, might approve.

10. The Ancient Town of Rye

In pre-Conquest days, when the coast of Rye and Winchelsea was very different in outline from today, King Canute granted the Manor of Rameslie to the Abbey of Fécamp. This comprised the area of Rye and Winchelsea. Why he should have done this seems obscure until it is realized that his predecessor, King Ethelred 'the Unready', had sought refuge at the Abbey of Fécamp in Normandy in 1014, when forced by the Danes to relinquish the throne of England. During this time he vowed that should he regain his throne he would grant an English Manor to this Abbey in Normandy. He regained the throne but died in 1016—characteristically with his vow unfulfilled— and the reign of his son, Edmund Ironside, was so brief that fighting the Danes left no time for attending to his father's promise to Fécamp. Therefore it fell to Canute (whose Queen Emma was the former wife of Ethelred) to make the actual grant of land to the Abbey.

So it came about that for more than two centuries the sister towns of Rye and Winchelsea came under Norman monastic control. This was well enough until, with the loss of Normandy to the French in 1204, the waters of the Channel separated alien countries. Foreign ownership of this important part of the coast could represent a danger to the realm, and therefore, during the reign of Henry III (in 1247) both Rye and Winchelsea ceased to belong to the Abbey of Fécamp and became Crown property. It was not a question of seizure and expulsion of the monks but a negotiated exchange of lands by which the Abbot and monks of Fécamp received, instead, inland Manors which included the Manor of Cheltenham in Gloucestershire.

Rye is often described as a hilltop town, but compared with such towns in France and Tuscany, which literally perch on mountainous heights, this hardly applies. Its hilltop character is only in contrast to the flatness of the Marsh

37. **Cobbled Mermaid Street** is one of the most famous streets in Rye. The sign of the Mermaid Inn, where the notorious Hawkhurst Gang of smugglers used to foregather, is seen on the right.

from which it is approached, and as you take the road from Brookland to Rye the little town, crowned by its ancient church around which the mellow roofs cluster, does seem to rise up as unexpectedly as the inland cliffs behind the marshland.

In the Middle Ages this was a favoured position as far as the menace of the sea was concerned—although the eastern and lower part of the town was, in fact, devoured by the waves in 1340. On the whole, however, the sea was kind to medieval Rye, for the Great Storm of 1287, which submerged Old Winchelsea and crippled Romney as a port, resulted in the river Rother's changed course flowing to the sea at Rye, with all the advantages which this created. Through the centuries the old town has clung to its original upland site against which the sea could storm in vain; not so the French, whose attacks during the Hundred Years War of the fourtcenth/fifteenth centuries were ferocious—as were, of course, the English raids on the other side of the Channel.

Most terrible of all the French attacks on Rye was the raid of 1377, when the whole town was left a smouldering ruin. But revenge followed, for in 1378 a joint raid of retaliation was made by the men of Rye and Winchelsea, during which the church bells of Rye, which had been stolen by the French, were retrieved. To quote Fuller's description in *The Worthies of England*, the English raiders 'took all such prisoners who were able to pay ransome, and amongst the rest they took out of the steeple the bells and brought them to England, bells which the French had taken formerly from these towns, and which did afterwards ring the more merrily, restored to their proper place with addition of much wealth for the cost of their recovery'.

When the interminable Hundred Years War did at last come to an end prosperity returned to Rye, and by the early sixteenth century the town could claim one of the finest of the Cinque Port harbours. And when Queen Elizabeth I visited Rye in 1573 she was so well pleased with the town, and with her reception, that she honoured it with the title Rye Royal. But the sea, as a patron, was more important than the Queen, and already it was beginning to withdraw its favour, gradually receding from the town so that the harbour today is little more than a quiet creek.

The entrance to Rye from the north is by the imposing fourtcenth-century Land Gate—a splendid sight and fitting introduction to this picturesque old town which has retained so much of its early character and architecture. To my mind winter is the best time of all for a visit, for then the town's charm is especially potent—when the streets are almost empty and the flames of open fires are glimpsed behind venerable window panes. The only disadvantage of a winter visit is that the Museum and Lamb House are both closed at this time of the year.

38. Rye's fourteenth-century Land Gate, entrance to the town from the north.

It seems to me that the starting point for any description of Rye should be Lamb House (on the corner of West Street and Church Square), for this was the home of the most important family in the history of the town, the Lambs; they occupied the office of Mayor for what must be a record span of years. Then in 1897 Lamb House became the home of the great American writer, Henry James. But before reaching

39. Lamb House, the Rye home of the great American novelist, Henry James, from 1897 until his death in 1916.

Henry James's ownership there is the tale of the Lamb family to be recounted, part of which is a grisly tale indeed.

James Lamb built the house in the early 1720's, incorporating in its structure part of an earlier building. From then onwards, for several generations, the Lambs practically ruled Rye. Earlier, in 1713, James Lamb had become Deputy

Controller of Customs in Rye, and therefore, in this town where smuggling was part of the way of life, there were plenty of people who regarded him with unfriendly eyes. One of these was the butcher John Breads, who was also proprietor of the Flushing Inn and who kept his butchery in the yard at the back of the inn. Mayor Lamb, who was also Chief Magistrate, had fined Breads for selling underweight to his customers, and, since the Flushing Inn was a smugglers' haunt, it can be surmised that Breads may have had other causes for disliking the Magistrate and Deputy Customs Controller.

One evening the Lamb family were planning a celebration on the revenue sloop lying in the harbour, for this was to be the first voyage of James Lamb's son, newly recruited to the customs service. Breads knew that on his return the Magistrate would cross the churchyard to Lamb House, and there he waited. But James Lamb was unwell that night, and on meeting his brother-in-law, Allen Grebell, he asked him to attend on his behalf. The night was dull and rainy, so he lent Grebell his cloak to save him collecting his own. It was this cloak which was to cost Allen Grebell his life, for as he returned from the sloop around midnight Breads was waiting for him behind a tombstone in the churchyard—the route by which he knew the Magistrate would return to Lamb House. As Allen Grebell lived only a few steps away, this was his route too. When the familiar cloak came into sight, Breads sprang from his hiding-place and plunged his butcher's knife twice into his supposed enemy's back. Allen Grebell somehow made his way back to his house and sank into a chair before the fire; and here he was found dead in the morning, a pool of blood on the floor beside him.

To add to the drama of the story—one which has, indeed, a Henry James flavour about it—James Lamb was roused three times during the night by a dream in which his dead wife implored him to go and see if her brother were safe. Twice, on waking, he decided it was a dream, and slept again. The third time, when dawn was breaking, he became sufficiently uneasy to dress and cross to his brother-in-law's house, where the poor man was found to have bled to death.

The butcher had achieved nothing more than the murder of a man against whom he felt no enmity, and he was soon accused of the crime, for as a murderer he certainly lacked cunning. He had made himself conspicuous following the deed by heavy drinking and a noisy tour of the town declaring, for all to hear, that butchers should kill lambs! This useful clue was quickly followed up, and then his bloodstained butcher's knife was discovered in the churchyard. When pronounced guilty at his trial, he remained completely unrepentant—only regretting that he had chosen the wrong man. 'I did not mean to kill Mr. Grebell,' he said, turning towards James Lamb. 'It was you I meant it for, and I would murder you now, if I could.'

Breads was imprisoned in the great Ypres Tower which now houses the Rye Museum, and then he was hanged on the Salts, the flat area which lies below the Land Gate. But before he died—and this seems well in keeping with the lurid tale—he was allowed a last drink at his own tavern, the Flushing Inn. Later his body was hung in chains for all to see, and so it remained for 50 years. The gibbet was then removed and the chains, with what remained of Breads, deposited in a lumber room of the church; in the course of time, the bones were gradually removed by women who attributed to them a cure for rheumatism. All that was left, eventually, was the upper half of the murderer's skull supported in the top of the chains—which survives to this day as a somewhat unsavoury relic in the Town Hall.

An earlier and more edifying record of James Lamb's occupancy of Lamb House was the visit of King George 1 in 1725 when the King's ship, returning to England from Hanover, encountered so severe a storm that it came ashore at Camber. The unfortunate monarch had to walk all the way from the beach to Rye and was exhausted by the time he approached the town. On hearing of the royal arrival James Lamb (then Mayor) rode out to meet him, accompanied by a group of Jurats, and for the next few nights the King stayed at Lamb House, the visit lasting from 3 to 7 January 1725.

This was a most untimely moment for entertaining so illustrious a visitor, for soon after the King's arrival Mrs.

Lamb gave birth to a son. The child was baptized in St. Mary's Church, with the King graciously acting as Godfather and presenting his Godson with an inscribed silver bowl. The bowl was, at least, believed to be silver; when later, owing to a bit of financial embarrassment, it was sold, the bowl was found to be plated—so either the Rye silversmith tricked the King, or else George I had a thrifty streak.

Two of the Lambs of Rye, as Barons of the Cinque Ports, shared the honour of carrying the royal canopy at coronations. These were James Lamb at the coronation of George II and Queen Caroline of Ansbach in 1727; and William Phillips Lamb at the coronation of George IV in 1821.

The record of the Lamb family as Mayors of Rye totted up to most remarkable figures: James Lamb, 13 times; his eldest son Thomas, 20 times, and the younger son James, 7 times; his grandson Thomas Phillips Lamb, 20 times; great-grandson William Phillips Lamb (last bearer of the canopy), 10 times; the Rev. George Augustus Lamb, 7 times. In fact, it is recorded that, with 19 exceptions, the Lambs or their kinsmen occupied the Mayoral office from 1723 to 1832.

This monopoly was made possible by the state of local government which caused Rye to be classified as a 'Rotten Borough'. Not that there was anything very rotten about the Lambs, but the system of representation gave the people little chance of dislodging them from their position of power until the Reform Act of 1832. An attempt was made in the 1750's by an adventurous character from Winchelsea named Edwin Wardroper who, like the butcher Breads, nursed a sense of hatred towards the Lambs owing to dismissal from his appointment as Town Clerk of Rye. This battle, as might be expected, ended in total defeat for the disgruntled Wardroper. Seventy-five years later another effort to topple the Lamb bastion was carried out under the leadership of William Holloway, historian of Rye, and his wife's kinsman, John Meryon. The reformers occupied the Town Hall and elected their own Mayor, so that for a time Rye was in the unusual position of possessing two Mayors. The Lamb party again emerged victorious, but the Reform Act brought their power to an end.

Among the names of Members of Parliament for the borough the Lambs are, needless to say, prominent. But another name, much more celebrated, also appears in the Parliamentary record—that of Sir Arthur Wellesley, later Duke of Wellington and Lord Warden of the Cinque Ports.

It was in 1897 that Henry James came to live in Lamb House, and this was to be his favourite home until his death in 1916. His flat in London, where he died, was regarded only as the place to which he resorted if the cold of the Rye winter became too severe. Lamb House was the home he loved so well that he left it only with the deepest regret and returned with overwhelming eagerness after every period of absence. Here he was looked after by Burgess Noakes, who came initially as a young houseboy, remained to become valet, butler and the ever-loyal and devoted member of his staff who nursed him in his final illness. At the time of writing Burgess Noakes still lives in Rye.

One of Henry James's most cherished possessions at Lamb House was the detached Garden Room whose great window provided an unrestricted view of the happenings of West Street. Here he worked every morning, and after his death, when his friend E. F. Benson occupied the house, it was from this window that the principal character of his novel, *Miss Mapp*, gained so absorbing a view of the goings-on of the town.

For those who like a ghost story, an interesting one is told of Lamb House and the Garden Room. E. F. Benson and the Vicar of Rye both saw (and both agreed in their description of what they saw) a man wearing a cloak who passed the garden entrance and then vanished into thin air: on another occasion a similar cloaked figure was seen in the Garden Room. This was assumed to be the spirit of the luckless Allen Grebell, wearing the cloak which was the cause of his death. Another ghostly anecdote concerns a tiny old lady who wore a mantilla and was seen by Henry James on many occasions; he seems, in fact, to have had an affection for this ephemeral companion and found her presence an aid to inspiration.

Hitler put an end to the days of the Garden Room and all its memories. In 1940 a direct hit demolished the little building completely, and today a plaque on the garden wall is all there is to recall its existence. The loss has taken with it one of the most evocative memories of Henry James's home in Rye.

The house was bequeathed to the writer's nephew, Henry James, Junior, of New York—who, incidentally, married the sister of Ruth Draper, famous for her stage 'monologues', if that word can convey the brilliance of her single-handed performances. The brothers A. C. Benson and E. F. Benson then shared tenancy of the house until, on the death of its owner, it was donated to the National Trust. Henry James's kinsman, H. Montgomery Hyde (author of *The Story of Lamb House, Rye*, and of *Henry James at Home*) then lived there until he left Rye. The present tenant, continuing the literary tradition of the house, is the novelist Rumer Godden, whose enchanting *Greengage Summer* is possibly the most famous of all her works.

Although the whole of Lamb House is not open to the public, the Henry James Room can be visited on two afternoons a week during summer. Here are relics and mementoes, together with the rather sparse remains of his library. This was badly damaged by the 1940 bomb, and many of the books which survived were sold on the death of Henry James, Junior, in 1948. Those which remain are not, therefore, typical of Henry James's library during his lifetime. There are first editions of his works, however, and also some of the volumes which his many literary friends sent to him when their own works were published.

The Henry James Room is what he used to describe as the Telephone Room. It leads directly off the entrance hall, and when it acquired its title this was not so humdrum as it sounds, for Henry James was among the early owners of a telephone for domestic use. In the hall is Kneller's portrait of George I—a reminder of the King's unheralded visit to the Lambs.

Lamb House presents an enigmatic face to West Street, and therefore the lightness and charm of its interior are all the more emphatic when the front door opens. This entrance door is massive, and possesses a fine Georgian knocker which is a curiosity in itself, for when lifted it operates automatically the latch inside. The hall is beautifully proportioned, and the garden a delight. Henry James loved this garden, as did the two Bensons—and as, obviously, does its present owner, Rumer Godden. In a corner of the garden is a small dogs' cemetery where plaques commemorate the pets of Henry James and E. F. Benson. One of E. F. Benson's dogs was a particularly familiar sight in Rye, and is still to be seen, in a corner of the stained glass west window in St. Mary's Church; his master also appears in the window, in Mayoral robes, for E. F. Benson was Mayor of Rye for three successive years and it was during his period of office that the window was erected in memory of his father, Edward Benson, Archbishop of Canterbury. The south window commemorates A. C. Benson, also of Lamb House, who was Master of Magdalene College, Cambridge, and he, too, is portrayed in the stained glass.

The reason for the unexpected spaciousness of the garden at the back of Lamb House is that it was originally a Deese (the Sussex word for a yard where bloaters or herrings were dried).

It is only a few steps from Lamb House to the famous Mermaid Street—steep and cobbled and so charming that its picture appears, with steady regularity, on calendars, Christmas cards, and in every book on the area. It would be difficult to find a more delightful street anywhere; but this is where my recommendation for winter exploration of Rye yields special dividends, for in summer throngs of visitors make their way along Mermaid Street, and only when it is almost empty does its special appeal become apparent.

The Mermaid Inn is almost as well known as the street in which it stands. Although its frontage has been restored the inn is basically fifteenth century, with cellars that go back to medieval times.

On the opposite side of Mermaid Street to the Inn is Jeake's House, or Jeake's Storehouse, as it was originally classified. The family of Jeake was prominent in Rye for generations, and each of the three Samuel Jeakes—father, son and grandson—was a considerable personality. Samuel Jeake the First, a man of great learning, has enjoyed the most permanent fame, for his work *Charters of the Cinque Ports, Two*

F

Ancient Towns and Their Members, published in 1728, is still the standard work on the subject. Indeed, he studied his subject so thoroughly that his footnotes have been described as more copious than the charters themselves—which is, of course, what one requires if any idea is to be gained of the contents of these early charters. He was a keen astrologer and took no risks in the building of his house, ensuring that the first stone was laid when the heavens augured well. His son, Samuel Jeake the Second, seems also to have had a phenomenal list of talents, and like his father he was an astrologer. The third Samuel Jeake invented a flying machine which remained stubbornly earthbound and was, for a time, stored in Peacock's Grammar School in the High Street.

The literary heritage of Jeake's House was continued in the present century when it became the home, in the 1920's, of the famous American novelist and poet Conrad Aiken. During the time that he lived there it became a gathering place for writers and artists—among them T. S. Eliot, Julian Huxley, Dame Laura Knight, Robert Nichols, Paul Nash and Edward Burra. Conrad Aiken's son, John Aiken—also a successful writer—has told me that one of his most lasting memories of childhood in Rye was going to Lamb House as a small boy to play chess with E. F. Benson.

Almost opposite Jeake's House is the fine half-timbered Old Hospital, or Hartshorn House, which became the property of Samuel Jeake the Second as part of the dowry of his 13-years'-old bride, Elizabeth Hartshorn. During the Napoleonic Wars it was used as a hospital, hence the name.

Watchbell Street is the other special showpiece among Rye's thoroughfares. It is, in fact, my favourite, for it has a pleasing sense of spaciousness and dignity in addition to its antiquity. The name derives from the watch which was kept here for the approach of French raiders, and the bell was rung if they were sighted.

Watchbell Street leads into Church Square, truly one of the loveliest parts of Rye with its many half-timbered houses and its crowning glory, the grand old church of St. Mary. This is the church which Samuel Jeake the First described as 'the goodliest edifice of its kind in Kent or Sussex, the

40. Watchbell Street vies with Mermaid Street for charm. In the old days Rye's watchman manned the look-out post here and rang a bell if French raiders were sighted.

cathedrals excepted'. Jeake was a dedicated 'Ryer' and therefore prejudiced, for there are other superb churches in these counties. Nevertheless, there is a quality about St. Mary's that is exceptional. Its most famous feature is the clock, claimed to be one of the oldest parish church clocks with its original works still functioning, and a distinguishing feature is the massive pendulum which swings backwards and forwards within the church. Outside, the gilded Quarter Boys (an addition of 1760 and renewed in 1970 when the earlier versions began to disintegrate) provide a constant attraction for visitors. They strike the quarters, *not* the hours. Between the Quarter Boys are the words from the Wisdom of Solomon in the Apocrypha, 'For our time is a very shadow that passeth away'.

It is well worth climbing to the top of St. Mary's tower, not only for the view gained but also to see the works of this grand old clock. This is only possible on weekdays in summer, for the tower is closed in winter and on Sundays. The church

41. **The gilded Quarter Boys** on the tower of St. Mary's Church strike the quarters but not the hours. They are a constant source of interest to Rye's visitors.

is of Norman origin, its chancel dating from 1120, the nave from 1180, and aisles from a slightly later period. The whole church was, however, left a smouldering ruin by the French raiders of 1377. The Norman font is a loss, too, for it is to be found over the county border, in the church at Newenden, Kent; the Rye font is a nineteenth-century copy. It seems sadly amiss that the original should be so near and yet be lost to St. Mary's. In the St. Nicholas Chapel is the tomb of Allen Grebell, whose epitaph relates his death at the hands of the 'sanguinary butcher' in 1742.

On the north-west corner of Church Square is an old house whose chimney stack is the source of much amazement to passers-by, for this is one of the crookedest chimneys likely to be seen in many a long year. At the foot of the stack is a

42. This crooked chimney in Church Square belongs to Grene Hall, the house where Queen Elizabeth I is believed to have been entertained during her visit to Rye in 1573.

doorway which leads into the ancient barrel-vaulted cellar. This building was once known as Grene Hall, and then as the Custom House; it became the home of James Lamb's son, the second James, when his elder brother, Thomas, was

43. Rye's Water House, in the churchyard of St. Mary's, was built in 1735 for the purpose of bringing pure spring water to the old town on the hilltop.

heir to Lamb House. Although many features are of a later period, this house dates back to the fifteenth century and Queen Elizabeth I is said to have been received here on the occasion of her visit in 1573. Another fifteenth-century house of striking appearance is the half-timbered St. Anthony, on the corner of Watchbell Street and Church Square. The oldest house in the square is, however, the Old Stone House, which dates from the thirteenth century and is one of the very few buildings in Rye which survived the burning and pillaging of the 1377 raid. Originally it formed part of a friary established in the 1260's by a Mendicant Order, the Friars of the Sack.

A curious little brick building which should not be over-looked is the Water House in St. Mary's Churchyard. This was built in 1735 and has a very individual charm. Rye always had a good supply of pure water from its wells and springs beneath the hill area, and the intention in building the Water House was to provide an equally pure water supply for the people of the old town at the higher level. Pipes were laid to pump it from the foot of Conduit Hill, but that it would be equally pure by the time it reached its destination proved a forlorn hope in the eighteenth century, owing to the proximity of the butchers' quarter in Market Street. In 1754, for instance, several calves' feet were found in the supposedly pure con-tents of the Water House, and a reward was offered for in-formation leading to the capture of any future saboteurs of the town's water supply.

Market Street, as will be remembered, was where the 'sanguinary butcher' had his yard at the back of the Flushing Inn. This inn, in addition to its ancient barrel-vaulted cellar, is also of interest in having a sixteenth-century wall painting which occupies the whole of one side of the front dining-room. Considering the Flushing Inn's old-time smuggling reputation, it is an amusing twist of fate that the adjacent building, which once formed part of the inn, is now in the hands of the law instead of the lawless; it is occupied by a firm of solicitors!

One of the best smuggling stories of this Rye and Winchelsea area might have been Thackeray's *Denis Duval*, for the story was building up engrossingly when the great Victorian novel-ist died. We shall never know the adventures that were in store for Denis, his crafty old smuggling grandfather, and the suave smuggler, the Chevalier de la Motte; but the atmosphere of Rye and Winchelsea at the end of the eighteenth century, with the stealthy night forays of the smugglers and highwaymen, is admirably conveyed. The Old Grammar School in the High Street at Rye, built in 1636 and founded by Thomas Peacock, is where Denis Duval received his education; it is thinly masked as Pocock's School in the novel.

Among Rye's literary associations it is astonishing that a 'new' book by Beatrix Potter, with the Ancient Town as its setting, should have been published as recently as 1971. By

44. Where the murderer Breads had his butcher's yard. This little street at the back of the Flushing Inn is part of Church Square. It leads from Market Street to the Ypres Tower.

new, of course, I mean in its present form, for *The Tale of the Faithful Dove* was written by Beatrix Potter in 1907; she hid it away and it did not re-emerge until after her death. She never illustrated it and therefore, although a small edition was published without the delight of her illustrations, the tale and its characters never became a nursery favourite as did the rest of her books.

Only in 1971 has this, one of her most charming tales, made its appearance with illustrations by Marie Angel that are, without any element of copying, as delightful as anything that Beatrix Potter herself would have done, and completely in the mood of her tale. All these years later, therefore, we become acquainted with Mr. Tidler and his wife Amabella who, despite the title of the book, seem to be a couple of everyday pigeons. Their adventures are set in Church Square, Mermaid Street and the summit of the Ypres Tower where they roosted and where Mr. Tidler bobbed and bowed in admiration of Amabella.

Rye's High Street is today the busiest part of the town and caters for the daily shopping of Ryers for food and household goods. In the days when cars were less prolific Ellen Terry used to drive into Rye in her pony-trap from her cottage in Winchelsea (her country home before she acquired Small-hythe Place). The story is told that she would bring the pony to a halt in the High Street, whereupon the local draper would carry out a selection of hats for her to try on—which she would do, sitting in the trap and viewing herself in a mirror held aloft by the obliging draper.

The fourteenth-century Land Gate is the sole survivor of the original gates in the town wall, and imposingly massive it is. Older by a century is the great Ypres Tower, known originally as the Baddings Tower, which stands solidly and austerely in the Gun Garden, gazing out over the Town Salts to the river Rother and the Marsh. It was constructed during the reign of Henry III, when so many of the coastal defences were strengthened, but by 1430 the fortunes of Rye were in decline and the town was reduced to converting its fortified Baddings Tower into money; it was sold to a private owner, John de Ypres, whose name it has borne ever since.

45. The thirteenth-century Ypres Tower was originally known as the Baddings Tower and was part of the coastal defences built by Henry III. It became the property of John de Ypres in the fifthteenh century, hence its name. The Ypres Tower now houses the Rye Museum.

In 1518, when good times had returned, the town repurchased the tower, which then became the courthouse and jail—to which, in a later century, the butcher Breads was consigned, as already related.

Today the Ypres Tower houses the Rye Museum, whose contents we are lucky to be able to see at all, for its former home, Battery House, received a direct hit during the last war. The building was completely destroyed, but a good number of the exhibits were salvaged, and the collection was eventually reassembled in the Ypres Tower. Considering its vicissitudes, this is a fascinating collection in a most unusual setting, many of the exhibits being displayed in recesses entered by low stone doorways—once the retention cells. Many additions to the collection have been made during the years since Hitler's bomb, so that the museum has probably even more to show now than before.

Of special interest are the Cinque Ports exhibits. These include a portion of the canopy carried by the Barons over Queen Charlotte at the coronation of George III in 1761, together with one of the silver-gilt bells which ornamented the staves. The breeches, hat, shoes and sword of a Rye Baron of the Cinque Ports at this coronation are displayed, together with an elegant Baron's waistcoat; there are also uniforms and weapons of the Cinque Ports Volunteers dating from the time of the Napoleonic threat.

Among items of local interest is a fascinatingly primitive hand-operated fire engine used in Rye between 1745 and 1865. This produced a stream of water of such weak force that the wooden apparatus had to be placed dangerously near to the flames, at risk of adding to the conflagration. It seems remarkable that this exhibit, one of the oldest fire engines of its type, has survived to tell the tale.

There are some good examples in the museum of the nineteenth-century work of the Rye Pottery. These have a curious and very characteristic ornamentation of hops and hop leaves which makes them immediately identifiable once you have learnt to recognize the style.

From the parapet of the Ypres Tower there is a view across to another tower, and this, I was told, is where the women prisoners were detained; the small lawn in between was once the exercise yard of the prison. Anyone leaning over the parapet edge today, when looking in this direction, will see below two small entrance doors, approached by steps, and these were the solitary confinement cells. The widespread view from the parapet embraces the Town Salts and stretches away towards the Marsh, while the river Rother can be seen winding along its placid path as it flows to the sea at Rye Harbour; mingling with it, in the foreground of the view, are the joint waters of the rivers Brede and Tillingham.

There are a number of potteries in Rye. This is a craft which dates far back in the history of the town, for an important pottery existed in medieval times until the Black Death of the fourteenth century brought it to an end. Today the most famous is the one which bears the name of the town—the Rye Pottery founded in 1869, where the brown and green Sussex rustic ware was produced, with its great swags of hops and hop leaves as ornamentation. This is no longer made, for it has been replaced by present-day designs, and the nine-teenth-century rustic ware has now gained collectors' piece status.

In the flat countryside between the town of Rye and Rye Harbour is Camber Castle, one of Henry VIII's string of Tudor Rose fortresses which are described in greater detail in the chapter on Deal and Walmer. Rye Harbour itself is a strangely small-scale relic of the once great maritime import-ance of this Cinque Port; it is rather bleak and muddy in winter, but gay with yachts and other small boats at week-ends in summer, and usually attracts a sprinkling of artists at their easels. Another Rye outpost is Rye Foreign—a name which tends to mystify visitors until it is realized that 'in the Foreign' meant in the area outside the jurisdiction of the Cinque Ports.

In the sixteenth century considerable numbers of French Huguenot refugees settled in Rye and Winchelsea, and the historian William Camden (1551–1623) recorded that 'Eliza-beth entertained with all kind of courtesy such French people as fled into England; as also the Netherlanders of whom a great multitude had withdrawn themselves into England, as to sanctuary, while the Duke of Alva breathed nothing but death and blood against them . . .' Following the Massacre of St. Bartholomew in 1572 as many as 641 Protestant refugees from France are said to have sought refuge in Rye in three days alone.

I am going to end this description of Rye by returning to the very centre of the town, for I have not yet mentioned the Town Hall in Market Street from which, on the occasion of the Mayoring each May, the newly elected Mayor throws showers of hot pennies—a tradition much appreciated by the children of Rye. It is an eighteenth-century building of great architectural charm, with its arcaded front and a cupola which rises gracefully over the roofs of the old town and competes with the church tower as a landmark. Here the fine maces are kept—for the Mayor of Rye is in the rare position of being preceded on official occasions by *two* maces, a right which dates back to the days of government by both Mayor and King's Bailiff, each having his own mace. Today the two offices are combined, but the Mayor still has both maces. They are extremely fine, and served as model for the design of the mace for Canada's House of Commons in Ottawa.

In the Town Hall, too, are the chains from which the macabre remnant of the butcher Breads still peers forth—a reminder that butchers should *not* always kill lambs.

11. Winchelsea—A Medieval 'New Town'

Winchelsea is today the most peaceful and calm of all the Confederation Ports. It seems almost as if the fates decided that this town, which suffered so terribly from storm and attack in its earlier history, should now enjoy exceptional tranquillity. To drive into Winchelsea from Rye in the quiet of the evening is to feel transported into a new world, to discover what the poet Coventry Patmore meant when he described it as 'a town in a trance'. During the day, in summer, visitors throng into Winchelsea and the lull is broken, but in the evening, or in the months of spring, autumn and winter, this trance-like spell returns.

The road that stretches between Rye and Winchelsea is not attractive. The picturesque cobbled streets of Rye have been left behind and this couple of miles across the flats, apart from the view of Camber Castle on the seaward side, has little charm. Then suddenly the road soars up a steep hill, a great expanse of marshland spreads out before the eyes, and the ancient Strand Gate leads into Winchelsea.

There is no trace of the Saxon island-town of Old Winchelsea, submerged in the Great Storm of 1287; this was located to the east, where the Camber Sands now lie. It apparently enjoyed greater importance in its day, as town and port, than the new town on the heights ever succeeded in regaining. For instance, on William I's journey back to England in 1067 (after returning to Normandy following the Conquest), it was to Old Winchelsea that he sailed.

By the beginning of the thirteenth century (the century that was to bring its downfall) Old Winchelsea had reached the height of its power as a trading centre, port, and anchorage for vessels of the Cinque Ports fleet. It had two churches dedicated to St. Thomas and to St. Giles (dedications repeated in the new town, following the inundation), a monastic house of the Franciscans, and it was described as 'a pretty town';

another account says that it had, according to tradition, as many as 50 inns and taverns.

The final tempest of 1287 completed the onslaught of previous storms which, as early as 1250, had demolished 300 houses and several churches, providing ample warning of the old town's peril. According to Leland, writing in the sixteenth century, 'The oulde Toune of Winchelesey of a vi or vii yeres together felle to a very soore and manifest ruine be reason of old rages of the se.' In fact, five years before the total disaster a Commission, headed by King Edward I's Treasurer and the Mayor of London, had been sent to Old Winchelsea to investigate the town's danger. Their report recommended its abandonment—that a new town should be built on higher and safer ground. The site chosen was 150 acres on the heights of Iham, and the removal was to be gradual and orderly.

But the Great Storm of 1287 took no notice of recommendations and plans. It broke with catastrophic force, and when it had died away Old Winchelsea, as a flourishing town and port, had vanished for ever. The inhabitants took refuge on the heights of the Iham peninsula (where the present town stands) and here, in the following year, the people assembled to listen to the words of the King's emissary, John de Kirkeby, Bishop of Ely and Treasurer of England, and to learn how the new town was to be planned and divided.

This 'new town' was a fascinating example of medieval town planning. It was developed on a grid-iron principle of straight roads which criss-crossed and provided plots of land based on previous holdings in the old town. On these, dwellings and business premises were to be built, for the wine trade between Winchelsea and France was an important sphere of activity at this time, and to this day great wine cellars survive beneath many of the houses; these were to provide ideal 'hides' for smugglers' contraband in later centuries.

In about 1290 the Church of St. Thomas the Martyr was founded by Edward I, its site allocated in the original plan so that this superb building would form the centre-piece of the new town. A second but smaller church, St. Giles, stood to the south-west, but this has completely disappeared. Roads and wharves were constructed, town walls built, and the harbour developed where the northern shore of the Iham peninsula was washed by the river Brede—a much greater river then than its present width indicates. Although no trace survives of the town walls, the extent of the original plan can be judged today by the surviving gates.

The Strand Gate I have already mentioned. This was the entrance to 'new' Winchelsea from the port area; the Pipewell Gate was, and still is, located on the road to Udimore, little more than 400 yards from the Strand Gate; but it is the position of the New Gate, on the road to Pett, that is so surprising. The New Gate was, of course, 'new' only in medieval times, and this remote archway in its meadowland setting indicates the extent of the plans for the thirteenth-

46. **King Edward I,** founder of the new town of Winchelsea after Old Winchelsea was submerged in the Great Storm of 1287. This sculptured portrait is in the Alard Chantry of St. Thomas's Church.

century town; but no trace of early dwellings survives here, and it is not certain that all the plots allocated were ever fully built upon. In the centre of the town, however, construction went ahead with speed. The dwellings were mainly of wood, and only the churches, monastic houses, town walls and the massive gates were built of stone.

Edward I's personal interest in the design and building of

the new town provides testimony of his tolerance and states-
manship, for within his own memory the seamen of Old
Winchelsea, and of the Cinque Ports in general, had been far
from loyal to the reigning house, having sided strongly with
Simon de Montfort and the Baronial Party in the Civil War of
1258–65.

In 1297 an incident occurred which gave Edward 1 an
almost legendary reputation in the eyes of the people of
Winchelsea. The King was preparing to sail for Flanders and
had come to the town to view his fleet, lying in the harbour
there. For this purpose he rode towards the walled escarpment
above the harbour—where one of the town's windmills was
grinding busily. The noise and the whirling sails upset the
King's horse, and it refused to advance until, when whip
and spurs were used, it shot forward, leapt the wall and disappeared over the cliff edge. The fall was substantial, but the
horse landed on a mud-softened road, somehow remained up-
right and slithered forward another 12 feet. The King, with
superb horsemanship, retained his seat, turned the horse
round and rode back along the road into the town—where he
was greeted with joy and amazement. The incident is recorded
by Thomas of Walsingham as 'the miracle of the King's
salvation', and a house at the end of Castle Street, named 'The
King's Leap', still marks the spot.

The town's next century of disaster was during the reign
of Edward III, the reign which brought the Hundred Years
War and the mighty victories in France of Poitiers and
Crécy—but nevertheless subjected the towns of England's
south-east coast to retaliatory raids of terrible ferocity. Ill-
fortune had already struck in the 1320's when the Black Death
swept through the town. Raids by the French began in 1337,
when about 100 dwellings were burnt to the ground.

Winchelsea's most terrible raid, as far as sheer brutality was
concerned, was in 1359. On 15 March a fleet of considerable
size entered the harbour and about 3,000 Frenchmen landed
and broke into the town, the raid being so timed that the
townspeople were congregated in the Church of St. Giles,
celebrating Mass. The French set fire to the houses and burst
into the church, where such scenes of slaughter, rape and

desecration took place as can rarely have been enacted within sacred walls. But these men were wild and uncontrollable, and many had scores to settle.

The massacre in the Church of St. Giles has been described by two Chroniclers, Thomas of Walsingham and Henry of Knighton, and a ghastly tale it is. William Durrant Cooper, in his *History of Winchelsea* (1850) records the former's version of the disaster: '. . . after butchering many of the congregation and despoiling the church, they met with one woman of more beauty than the rest of her neighbours, and had come there together with them to her devotions; her the brutes seized upon, and, in that very place, most grossly assaulted, one after another, till the woman died.' Cooper continues: 'Henry of Knighton says that there were nine illustrious women ravished; that the French killed 40 townsmen; and that 400, who came to the succour of the town, were drowned in the harbour, out of which the French took 13 ships well freighted with wine and victuals. According to Leland, they stayed in the town a day and a night, and then returned to their ships, but were obliged to leave two behind, being fast in land.'

When the French sailed away the scene left behind was grim indeed, and the lane where the dead bodies lay before burial in St. Giles's graveyard is still known as Dead Man's Lane. So great was the disaster that the graveyard had to be enlarged to cope with the burials.

The townspeople had hardly had time for a semblance of recovery when the French landed again, on 15 March 1360— exactly one year later and on the anniversary of the previous massacre (assuming that Thomas of Walsingham was correct, for Henry of Knighton recorded a different date for the previous raid). Again scenes of great brutality took place, and after slaughtering every man they encountered in the town, the raiders swept through the neighbouring Ports and countryside, burning and pillaging. The Cinque Ports Fleet made a reprisal raid from Winchelsea in the same year—burning and pillaging, we can be sure, with equal ferocity. It was not a gentle age.

In 1377 came the raid during which Rye was burnt to the ground, but Winchelsea was saved by the defence of the stalwart Abbot of Battle who came to the town's rescue. On hearing that Rye had been occupied by the French, it is recorded that the Abbot put all his men into armour to defend the neighbouring villages; and when the enemy reached Winchelsea the defences were so well prepared that they retired again to Rye, thereupon setting fire to the town and reducing it to ashes. It was in the following year that the joint retaliatory raid by the men of Rye and Winchelsea retrieved the church bells which had been carried away in 1377.

In 1380 Winchelsea suffered another French raid which brought fire and terror, and this was when the Pipewell Gate was destroyed (not to be rebuilt until 1404, twenty-four years later). This was a highly organized attack under the leadership of the French Admiral, Jean de Vienne, whose men broke into the town by the New Gate. Winchelsea was burned, as were also the neighbouring Ports of Rye and Hastings, and the town of Appledore.

With the end of the long period of conflict and misery caused by the Hundred Years War, good fortune might have been expected to return to Winchelsea; but this was when the town's oldest enemy renewed its vendetta. The sea, which had earlier invaded and submerged Old Winchelsea, now withdrew, and by the end of the fifteenth century the town's life as an important port had ended. Slowly the scene changed, marshland lay where the ships had harboured, and with the port gone the merchant trade which had brought prosperity dwindled and disappeared. In the Elizabethan era Sir Walter Raleigh spoke of Winchelsea as 'gone to decay'; in the seventeenth century John Evelyn, following a visit to Winchelsea, recorded that from its former importance the town had become 'all rubbish', and that 'the sea, which formerly rendered it rich and commodious, hath now forsaken it'; and John Wesley, in 1790, referred to 'that poor skeleton of Ancient Winchelsea'.

Although trade had deserted the town and the buildings were decaying, the great cellars still existed where the merchants had stored their wines; and whereas the old legitimate wine trade with France had died away, a new trade in wine was thriving—the stealthy, moonlit trade of the smugglers, for which the cellars offered ideal hiding-places.

John Wesley came to preach in the new Wesleyan Chapel which had opened its doors in 1786, and on 7 October 1790 Winchelsea was the scene of the last open-air sermon he was to give. He wrote in his diary (in addition to his 'skeleton' comment), 'I stood under a large tree on the side of it (St. Thomas's Church) and called to most of the inhabitants of the town, "The Kingdom of Heaven is at hand. Repent and believe

47. The former detached bell-tower of St. Thomas's Church which was demolished in 1790.

the Gospel." It seems as if all that heard were, at the present, almost persuaded to be Christians.'

Perhaps the Winchelsea townspeople felt that they could smuggle and be Christians too, for it is unlikely that the cellars were less well stacked with contraband that night than at any other time. The tree is still pointed out as Wesley's Tree, but it is, in fact, a descendant of the original.

The Church of St. Thomas the Martyr still dominates the little town, just as Edward I always intended it to do when he selected the site in the town plan. It is part parish church, part ruin, for the surviving section (70 feet in length) is little more than the original chancel with its side chapels; but the magnificence of this chancel is testimony of the splendour of the

48. St. Thomas's Church. In Edward I's plans for the new town of Winchelsea this church occupied a dominant position in the centre of the town. It still stands there, but the church today represents only the surviving chancel and side chapels of the original building.

church when completed—if, in fact, it ever was finally completed. The very explicit guidebook on sale in the church tells us that, at the time of its construction, the great oak timbers for the roofs came from the dense Forest of Anderida which formed an almost impenetrable barrier inland from the southern coastal towns; that Caen stone was brought from Normandy and marble from West Sussex; and at low tide the sea was gracious enough to surrender the battered but usable stones from the old town. This great church was built early in the century which followed the Great Storm of 1287, and it has been suggested that the nave was actually never completed. However, the nave foundations were excavated in 1790 and

49. Effigy of Sir Gervase Alard, Admiral of the Cinque Ports, in the Alard Chantry of St. Thomas's Church. He is clasping his heart in his hands.

fragments of tessellated flooring were unearthed—which would not have been laid until the roof was in position. William Durrant Cooper believed that the nave was burnt to the ground during the French raid led by Admiral Jean de Vienne in 1380.

It is the fine proportions and spaciousness of St. Thomas's that make the first overwhelming impression, and then the beauty of individual features becomes apparent. Most treasured of all are the effigied tombs of the Alard and Farncombe Chantries. The Alards were a Saxon family of pre-Conquest Sussex origin, and the figure in armour nearest to the altar is attributed to Gervase Alard, Admiral of Edward 1's Western Fleet and the first Portsman known to have borne the title

50. The fine carved sedilia in St. Thomas's Church.

of Admiral of the Cinque Ports. The hands clasp his heart, and among foliage of the canopy are seen the carved heads of Edward i and his second Queen, Margaret of France.

There have been two theories concerning the second tomb: one, that this is the effigy of Gervase's grandson, Stephen Alard, founder of the Chantry and also Admiral of the Cinque Ports and of the Western Fleet; secondly, that this is the effigy of an Oxenbridge who married into the Alard family. The former theory seems much more acceptable, for the Oxenbridge family was not on the same scale of importance as the Alards in these early days, and so prominent a burial place would obviously have been allocated to the founder of the Chantry. Although the tombs in the north wall bear the name of the Farncombe Chantry, the three canopied effigies have never been identified; they are believed to be older than the church itself and to have been saved from the wreckage of Old Winchelsea. The tomb of Gervase Alard forms the background of one of the most famous of Victorian paintings by Sir John Everett Millais (1829–96); this was one of his child paintings which now seem so over-sentimental but were immensely popular in his day.

Especially notable are the elaborately carved sedilia, and also of interest is an illustration within the church of the Great Seal of the Winchelsea Corporation, with a descriptive note which merits study. The device of the Counter Seal bears a representation of St. Thomas's Church with nave, side aisles, central tower and spire with crocketed gables and pinnacles; on the left is the vanished Church of St. Giles, and in the centre an embattled tower and lighthouse; a figure with lantern stands on the central tower, as if guiding ships into port. Three niches depict the martyrdom of St. Thomas, and buildings at the foot of the seal depict the religious houses which were established in 'new' Winchelsea.

Of these religious houses only scanty ruins survive, the most considerable being the chapel of the Grey Friars (Franciscans) which can be glimpsed from the section of the Hastings road known as Monks Walk. The ruins are in the grounds of the mansion built in 1819 and formerly the home of Lord Blanesburgh, who was the donor of the series of stained glass windows in the church and the fine organ; this mansion is now a home for the elderly. The Franciscans were, as I mentioned earlier, already established in Old Winchelsea at the time of the inundation, and the monks rebuilt in the new town. The Black Friars did not come to Winchelsea until the new town was well established, but fragmentary remains beside Rectory Lane are all that can be seen today of this monastic house. Even less survives of St. John's Hospital, a religious foundation which cared for the old and infirm and which stood on the Icklesham road; it is now represented by a stark and roofless wall.

Winchelsea was amply supplied with fresh water wells but only one lay within the walls. A curious little building in Castle Street enshrouds the Town Well, and in it still hangs a

51. Older than the Church itself are these effigies in St. Thomas's. They are believed to have been saved from the submerged town of Old Winchelsea.

mayoral order which reads as follows: 'Notice is hereby given that this well is to be closed at 7 o'clock in the evening and opened at 6 o'clock in the morning, and to be closed all day on the Sabbath.' There must have been quite a gathering of citizens with buckets at the Town Well on Saturday evenings before seven o'clock.

Close to the Town Well in Castle Street is the house known as the Armoury. This name, together with that of nearby Barracks Square, is a heritage of the Napoleonic Wars, for here soldiers were stationed to man the defences.

The oldest building in Winchelsea is the Court Hall, which dates back in origin to the early days of the new town. It once comprised the jail as well as the Court Room. Here the traditional Mayoring takes place each Easter Monday, an ancient ceremonial which has not changed for nearly 700 years.

There is, in fact, a great deal that has not changed in Winchelsea. For instance, the perpetual rent of £14. 11s. 5¾d.,

52. **Winchelsea's medieval Court Hall,** where the Mayoring takes place each Easter Monday with traditional ceremony. The Court Hall now houses the Winchelsea Museum. This drawing is from William Durrant Cooper's *History of Winchelsea,* published in 1850, but the appearance of the Court Hall is little changed today.

ordered by King Edward 1 in the thirteenth century as interest on the loan for building the new town, is still collected each year; since decimalization, this amounts to a little over £14·50. It was, of course, of far greater value in Edward 1's day.

Winchelsea has twelve Freemen, and a man is a Freeman for life when once appointed—whether or not he still lives in the town, or even in Britain. At the time of writing only six of the Freemen still live in Winchelsea and one lives in Cyprus. What would happen if a general emigration of Freemen took place, and they all continued to live elsewhere to a ripe old age, is open to speculation. When the annual Mayoring comes along the new Mayor is elected by the Freemen from among the Freemen, and when there is a vacancy by death among their number, the new Freeman is appointed by the Mayor. Thus the Freemen elect the Mayor, and the the Mayor appoints each new Freeman.

53. The New Inn and some of the houses which face the church in the centre of Winchelsea.

This self-perpetuating governing body owns the ancient Court Hall and the three gates of the town; and when the Court Hall comprised the town jail, it owned the jail too. The Jurats are chosen from among the Freemen as the Mayor's working assistants, and their tasks include collection of the old rents for handing to the Crown. One delightful old house I visited has always paid an annual crown rent of $3\frac{3}{4}$d. (presumably now about $1\frac{1}{2}$p).

And so Winchelsea lives on with its customs almost unchanged. The Mayoring takes place each Easter Monday at eleven a.m., the ancient wording of the ceremony being the same as has been used 'time out of mind'. The Mayor, Jurats, Freemen and Town Clerk walk to the ancient Court

Hall, in procession, just as they have done through all the centuries.

This medieval Court Hall houses Winchelsea's little museum, and this is well worth visiting. Here, as in most of the Cinque Ports museums, are preserved the robes of a Baron of the Cinque Ports—in this case Winchelsea's Baron who attended the coronations of King George vi and Queen Elizabeth ii. There is a model showing the town as planned by Edward i, and a list of Mayors of Winchelsea covers an extensive area of the Court Hall walls. The names are grouped under the heading of each reigning monarch, the Cromwellian period appearing as 'The Interregnum'. A noticeable feature is the repetition of names in the Mayoral list—due to the fact that the Mayor can be chosen only from the 12 life-serving Freemen. The Winchelsea Common Horn lies in a case—formerly its notes summoned the Freemen to elect their new Mayor.

An interesting relic is a much-faded wall painting, on wood, which is believed to represent St. Leonard and to have come from the vanished Church of St. Leonard. St. Leonard's was not, in fact, a Winchelsea church, for it stood just outside the 'new town' walls and was the parish church of Iham. The great black windmill (near the Black Friars ruins) marks its site. This windmill stopped work in 1905 and lacks its sails (or 'sweeps', to use the Sussex term), but it is, nevertheless, a very distinctive feature of the town as it stands alone on its grassy mound with only the sheep to keep it company.

Among other exhibits in the museum is a collection of agricultural bygones, including a bull clamp 'for holding unruly bulls by the nose'; to me, it looks far too slight an implement to restrain even the mildest cow, let alone an unruly bull. A curiosity is the plaster cast of a footprint discovered after a landslide in 1957 at the foot of the cliff at Fairlight. No certainty is claimed for its origin, but it has been suggested that it could represent the footprint of an iguanodon—the same prehistoric dinosaur whose bones are preserved in the church at Stone-in-Oxney.

An item much closer to our own time but fascinating historically is the *History of the Shire of Winchelsea in Victoria*,

Australia, dated 12 June 1935, and sent to the citizens of Winchelsea, England, 'as a record of 78 years of progress in the 98th year of the settlement of the district, and to commemorate the centenary of our State'.

An American literary association with Winchelsea is that Conrad Aiken came to live at the Look Out Cottage with his first wife and young family from 1922 to 1924. It was after this period, when the cottage became too small and cramped for them, that they moved to Jeake's House in Mermaid Street, Rye. His son, John Aiken, whose memories of playing chess with E. F. Benson at Lamb House, Rye, are related in the previous chapter, also told me how clearly he remembers their arrival in Winchelsea for the first time—the entrancement, for a small American boy, of place names such as Appledore and Hamstreet as the leisurely little train puffed through these stations on its way to Winchelsea; and the magic of the great expansive view from Look Out Cottage across the Marsh and over the sea to France.

Almost opposite Look Out Cottage is Tower Cottage, which was the country home (prior to Smallhythe Place) of Dame Ellen Terry, and from here she would set out in her pony-drawn trap to do her shopping in Rye. She must have had steady nerves and good brakes for pony and trap not to run away with her on the steep hill from the Strand Gate.

As far as literary associations are concerned, Sheila Kaye-Smith's *The End of the House of Alard* tells of the family whose ancestral effigies lie, in stony calm, in the Alard Chantry in St. Thomas's Church; and the Winchelsea of the eighteenth-century smugglers was, as I have already mentioned, the setting for Thackeray's unfinished *Denis Duval*. Denis recalls how, in his boyhood, 'there were points for which our boats used to make, and meet the French boats when not disturbed, and do a great deal more business than I could then understand. From Dungeness to Boulogne is but six-and-thirty miles, and our boats, when war was over, were constantly making journeys there. Even in wartime the little harmless craft left each other alone, and, I suspect, carried on a great deal of peaceable and fraudulent trade together. Grandfather

54. **The Strand Gate** is approached by a steep incline and was, when built at the end of the thirteenth century, the entrance to Winchelsea from the port area.

had share of a "fishing" boat, with one Thomas Gregson of Lydd.'

Into this Protestant stronghold of Winchelsea, and into the very household of the Duvals (of French Protestant refugee descent) comes the Papist Clarissa de Saverne, to the great discomfiture of all. To Clarissa is born the child Agnes, who Denis loves and marries. Because of her religion Agnes is brought up at the Priory (obviously the Friars, the predecessor of the Grey Friars mansion of 1819 which became the property of Lord Blanesburgh, and in whose grounds still stand the

55. The Town Well in Castle Street. Only when piped water was brought to Winchelsea did the importance of this little building fade, for until then it was the only well available for public use within the town.

ruins of the Franciscan chapel). This house was the home of the brothers known as 'the notorious Westons'—in both the book and in real life.

These two disreputable characters, Joseph and George Weston, lived at the Friars, Winchelsea, from 1781–2, and their identity was concealed under the blameless names of William Johnson and Samuel Watson. They were described in the Annual Register as 'two of the most notorious villains who, for some years, have defrauded the country by various artful contrivances'. In Winchelsea their behaviour was irreproachable—away from Winchelsea they were engaged in the trade of the highwayman. But Joseph was not, according to the Sussex Archaeological Collections, at any time Churchwarden at Winchelsea, as has often been suggested; his cover-up righteousness did not go quite so far as that.

Eventually, as happened to most highwaymen in the end, the brothers were captured in London after holding up and robbing the Bath and Bristol mail coach between Maidenhead and Hounslow on 29 January 1781. They were sent to Newgate prison, escaped (aided by the two Weston wives), were recaptured and committed, additional charges now being added to their crimes—George Weston for forgery, Joseph Weston for shooting and wounding a passer-by at the time of his arrest. These two Winchelsea 'notabilities' met their end at Tyburn on 3 September 1782, and according to the appropriate issue of the *Gentleman's Magazine* they behaved most properly and penitentially at their execution.

56. **The Friars** at Winchelsea, from an old print of 1843. This mansion was built in 1819 on the site of the house which played a prominent part in Thackeray's unfinished novel, *Denis Duval*.

The Westons figure prominently in *Denis Duval*, and the hold-up of Denis's carriage *en route* for London by a highwayman who proves to be Joseph Weston is an important part of the plot. The house is as slightly disguised under its title of the Priory (instead of the Friars) as is Pocock's School (instead of Peacock's) at Rye.

57. Thirteenth-century Seal of the Corporation of Winchelsea, which dates from the early years of the reign of King Edward I.

Winchelsea Castle is occasionally referred to by past writers, and this can be baffling to visitors who find no trace of a castle at all. The solution is that Camber Castle, about one mile distant, used sometimes to be spoken of as Winchelsea Castle. This, one of Henry VIII's Tudor Rose Castles built in 1539, fell into decay, whereas Deal and Walmer continued to be used and in good repair. It is, however, far more intact than Sandgate, and in recent years has been undergoing restoration. Camber Castle was almost lost during the reign of King Charles I, for in 1626 the following order for its demolition was issued:

'That the King having been informed that "our Castle of Camber, in our county of Sussex, is grown into great decay, being forsaken by the sea and left distant from ye water two miles at the least, so as the same is now of no further use for defence, but of continual charge unto us, and being humbly

G

advised that our said castle should be demolished and the materials thereof sold to our use, and the value thereof employed for the fortifying of some other neighbouring castles and forts of more importance for our service and the safety of our kingdome, we do give full authority unto you, or any five or more of you, to sell the materials of the said Castle of Camber."'

For some reason or other the demolition order was not put into operation and this historic building survived.

One of the curiosities at Winchelsea (only discontinued in 1970) was the appointment of Keeper of the Look Out. The man who fulfilled this role, once so vital, earned the original sum of 5½d. a week, or about 2p decimal equivalent. But the sea had retreated so far from Winchelsea that keeping an eye open for the ships of likely invaders would need better eyesight than most of the elderly Keepers of the Look Out have been able to claim. Some years ago the holder of this appointment (in his seventies) caused quite a stir by asking the Mayor and Jurats if, in addition to his 5½d. a week, he could be provided with a telescope!

As will be gathered Winchelsea remains, for most months of the year, 'a town in a trance', just as the poet Coventry Patmore described a century ago. It is a trance that we can only hope will never be broken.

12. Hastings

The name of Hastings heads the list of the Cinque Ports, but although it remains coastal it is no longer a port; no harbour exists, and the fishing fleet is beached on the shingle. Yet in 1066, when William the Conqueror brought his army ashore at nearby Pevensey, the situation was very different, for the navigable creek and harbour at Hastings were strategic advantages well known to the invader.

The seaport continued to flourish after the Conquest, and in the twelfth century Hastings was supplying 20 ships to the King's Fleet, of which only two were contributed by its member towns of Winchelsea and Rye (not yet Head Ports in their own right). By 1229, however, the figures were already very different, for Hastings was providing a mere 6 ships against 10 from Winchelsea and 5 from Rye. By the time the Cinque Ports Confederation was approaching the greatest period of its power, with Edward I's Charter of 1278 confirming legally its services and privileges, Hastings was already in decline. The harbour was beginning to silt up, and the Great Storm of 1287, which destroyed Old Winchelsea and wrecked the prosperity of Romney, also dealt the death blow to Hastings as a port. Then the Hundred Years War of the fourteenth and fifteenth centuries brought raids and destruction by the French, and gradually this once great Cinque Port dwindled to the status of a small fishing town.

The men of Hastings did not submit easily to this state of affairs. Their sea power was of far too ancient standing to let it fade away without a fight. The very name of the Stade (the fishermen's quarter and foreshore of the Old Town) dates back to Saxon times and means landing-place. So, again and again throughout the centuries, efforts were made to build a new harbour and make Hastings once more a Cinque Port in the true sense of the title. But the sea won the day. The last attempt was in the 1890's, and the only surviving trace

58. Hastings as the Normans knew it. This reconstruction is by Gillian Betge and the original is in the Fishermen's Museum at Hastings.

of this projected harbour is the western arm which juts out into the sea, broken and battered, as the waves toss their spray against it.

No one pretends any longer that Hastings will be a great port again. But what matter, for the town has regained prosperity in other ways. It was in the eighteenth century that the new trend for sea bathing brought reprieve, and rapidly Hastings became a fashionable resort. By the nineteenth century the new seaside resort of St. Leonards was created to the west, and these two, once separated by a mile of countryside, have now merged to form the County Borough of Hastings with its three miles of promenade.

St. Leonards was the architectural achievement of a local builder, James Burton, and his more famous son, the architect Decimus Burton (who designed the Ionic screen at

Hyde Park Corner, London). They built on the grand scale, the principal feature being the now vanished Baths, with the Hydro opposite which survives today as the Royal Victoria Hotel. Behind lay the Pump Room, which has become the Masonic Hall, and behind this stretched the Subscription Gardens which have become the St. Leonards public gardens. The main residential section of this township was the Marina, which covered a distance of about 250 yards, with the Hydro as its centrepiece. A special feature was the planning of the front doors at the rear, which enabled the whole frontage to be devoted to window space and the sea view. Later, entrances from the Promenade were substituted, some of the back entrances were walled up, and others are today entrances to upper flats. Sad to say, much of the Burton dignity has disappeared and a certain drabness has attacked the buildings that survive, far removed from the pristine opulence of the St. Leonards of Burton's day; but the Royal Victoria Hotel (the erstwhile Hydro) remains in fine form, gleaming with white paint, and there is now hope for the other buildings, for a recently-formed St. Leonards Preservation Society has active plans for restoration and protection.

For most people, however, it is the Old Town of Hastings that holds the greatest attraction, and this area of topsy-turvy half-timbered houses and dignified Georgian and early Victorian buildings needs slow and thorough exploration if all its charms are to be discovered. On the front, the holiday crowds of summer, the cafés and refreshment kiosks, the fish and chip restaurants—and, alas, the motor coaches drawn up on the foreshore—can somewhat obscure the attraction; but wander along the High Street and All Saints Street, then turn along side roads and alleyways, and the appeal of the Old Town is very soon apparent. Even the fish and chip restaurants on the front fall into place, for this is still, despite the motor coaches, primarily the territory of the Hastings fishermen. Their harbourless boats are, as for long years past, hauled up the steep incline of the shore and beached on the shingle above the high water line—one of the very few fishing fleets in Britain to be so beached. Until 1936 they were hauled in by wooden capstans drawn by horses, but these are now worked by motor winches.

When walking eastwards along Hastings Promenade it is obvious that you are coming to the Old Town when the masts of the fishing craft and the tall 'net shops' of black-tarred timber come into view. These gaunt fishermen's huts are a real Hastings curiosity and are said to have originated in Elizabethan times or even earlier, though the present huts are thought to date from the early seventeenth century. There are

59. 'Net Shops' and the Fishermen's Museum on the foreshore at Hastings Old Town. There are over 40 of the net shops, most of which date from the seventeenth century and are still used for their original purpose of drying and storing the fishermen's nets.

43 of them and they stand at the top of the beach, some of the tallest three-storey huts rising to a height of about 30 feet. All still serve their original purpose. The word net shop, incidentally, is used in the same sense as workshop —a place for drying, mending and storing the nets.

It is remarkable that any of the net shops survive today, for during a June night in 1961 fire broke out among the closely-packed and highly-inflammable structures, and the scene rapidly became an inferno of flames and falling timbers. It seems almost miraculous that the fire was kept sufficiently under control to limit the loss to five net shops. These were carefully reconstructed with funds raised by public subscription, for the Old Town's foreshore without its net shops would be sadly bereft.

On the clifftop to the west of the Old Town are the remains of the Norman castle, which was built shortly after the Conquest to provide a stronger fortress than the one whose erection is depicted in the Bayeux tapestry (believed to have represented an example of Norman pre-fabrication).

After the Norman landing at Pevensey on 28 September 1066, William of Normandy moved eastwards to capture Hastings. A couple of weeks passed between the date of the landing and the final battle, and this enabled Harold, on 25 September, to defeat and slay England's other invader, Hardrada, King of Norway, at Stamford Bridge and to return south to tackle William's army, almost at its original landing-place. During this period, according to the Bayeux tapestry, the Norman soldiers occupied their time in burning down the homes of the luckless Hastings citizens.

On 14 October (Harold having brought his army south at great speed) the Battle of Hastings was fought in countryside seven miles to the north-west of Hastings itself. All day the mighty battle raged, and only as darkness was falling did the end come. Harold was slain, and where he fell William of Normandy later placed the altar of Battle Abbey, the monastic house which he built in pursuance of a vow made on the battlefield. And on Christmas Day, 1066, the Conqueror was crowned William I of England in Westminster Abbey.

Despite the somewhat fragmentary nature of the ruins, Castle

60. Building the first Norman Castle at Hastings, as depicted in the Bayeux Tapestry.

Hill should most certainly be ascended for it provides a superb view over the coastline and the Old Town; and out to sea the changed shading of the waters indicates the shallows where the original port of Hastings lies submerged. There are two ruins on this hilltop, for here, also, are the remains of the Collegiate Church of St. Mary, of which St. Thomas Becket was Dean and William of Wykeham a Canon. Separated from the castle mound by the vast ditch (which the Normans cut in order to make the castle impregnable, an operation also depicted in the Bayeux tapestry) is a grassy summit which once served as the tiltyard, and today it provides a marvellous viewpoint.

On descending to sea level again, it is best to start by exploring the Old Town's two principal streets, High Street and All Saints Street, both of which lead from the front and follow a short parallel route inland until they meet close to All Saints' Church. Between them a comparatively new road has been cut and this, except by the motorist, can be ignored. It is named the Bourne, after the stream which originally ran between the two old streets and which does, in fact, still flow beneath the

61. Shovells, the oldest house in Hastings, was the home of the mother of the seafaring Sir Cloudesley Shovell, who rose from cabin boy to Admiral and died when his ship was wrecked in 1707.

new road. The Bourne was first built over in 1835, and it is recorded that before this the stream had for centuries served as both drain and source of drinking water for the town. Obviously the higher and fresher water would have been used for the drinking water, but the combination does not sound attractive! As at Rye, appeals were made for informers in order to stop people depositing rubbish in the Bourne.

The idea of a new motor road slicing through the Old Town was, at first, rather intimidating, but it has released the two narrow streets from through traffic and rescued their houses, mainly half-timbered and Georgian (with a few jarringly-modern interlopers) from vibration and noise.

The oldest house is Shovells, a tiny half-timbered dwelling in All Saints Street where once lived the mother of the seafaring Sir Cloudesley Shovell (sometimes spelt Clowdisley). His is the tale of the poor boy who made good—who started as a shoemaker's apprentice, ran away to sea and eventually rose from cabin boy to admiral. He died a seaman's death when his ship, *Association,* was holed by rocks in dense fog off the Scilly Isles on 22 October 1707; the next day his body was washed ashore and he was buried in Westminster Abbey.

It is a happier episode in Sir Cloudesley Shovell's story that is recalled in the Old Town—the day when he ordered his ship to head for the Hastings coast so that he could be rowed ashore. He made his way to the tiny house in All Saints Street and, in answer to his knock, an old and obviously poor woman emerged. He kissed her, fell on his knees begging her blessing, and called her Mother. Their greetings were warm and affectionate, and, so the story goes, he gave her ten guineas and departed with tears in his eyes. Ten guineas bought a good deal more in his time than £10·50 does today, but one cannot help feeling that had he kept his eyes dry and sent her ten guineas more often she need not have appeared so poor and old. As we stand before Shovells today this little story does enable us to picture the door opening and the old woman coming out to greet her splendidly successful son, the admiral.

A number of famous names in literature, the arts and medicine have been associated with Hastings. Elizabeth Blackwell, Britain's first woman Doctor of Medicine, died at her home in Exmouth Place in 1910. Another pioneer of feminine achievement in the medical world was born in the Croft in 1840—Sophia Jex-Blake, founder of the London School of Medicine for Women.

62. Houses in Hastings Old Town which date back to Tudor times and are separated from the road by a raised pavement.

The great American artist James McNeill Whistler came frequently to Hastings to visit his mother, who lived in St. Mary's Terrace. It is said that his famous painting, *The Artist's Mother—an arrangement in Black and Grey*, which hangs in the Louvre in Paris, was wholly or partially painted at her window here. She is buried in Hastings cemetery.

Sir Rider Haggard (author of *King Solomon's Mines, She* and other well-known novels written towards the end of the nineteenth century) lived at North Lodge, St. Leonards, the house which forms an archway over Maze Hill. This arch was originally a tollgate in the days when the new and fashionable resort was deemed too exclusive for the admittance of all and sundry without payment of a toll. Sir Rider Haggard seems

63. Dickens Cottage in the High Street of the Old Town has no connection, it seems, with Charles Dickens or his novels. It is delightfully picturesque, however, in its own right.

to have had two completely separate sides to his character and work—his highly imaginative writing as a novelist, and his practical aspect as a barrister and authority on agricultural and social questions. One day, during the period when he was living in St. Leonards, he was invited to speak at a Rotary

Club luncheon in Hastings, and during question time he was asked how he reconciled these two totally different parts of his life—on the one hand, an authority dealing with hard facts, and on the other a writer of wildly romantic stories. He replied: 'When I am dealing with facts, I stick to facts; when I am writing stories, I stick at nothing.'

In the Old Town the dignified Georgian building entitled Old Hastings House was the home of the Victorian poet Coventry Patmore. It still stands at the spot where High Street and All Saints Street merge, its little cupola-ornamented garden room, or conservatory, adding greatly to its appeal.

Among literary visitors to the resort were Lord Byron and Charles Lamb, the latter writing, with somewhat jaundiced pen, on seaside resorts in general in *The Last Essays of Elia.* 'Old attachments cling to me in spite of experience,' he wrote. 'We have been dull at Worthing one summer, duller at Brighton another, dullest at Eastbourne a third, and are at this moment doing dreary penance at Hastings—and all because we were happy many years ago for a brief week—at Margate... I love town, or country; but this detestable Cinque Port is neither.' Charles Lamb was obviously out of sorts and had not bothered to seek out the charms of the Old Town; or it may be that the Old Town's appeal is especially apparent today, when much of modern architecture is charmless and shoddy and the old houses and alleyways seem all the more delightful by contrast.

The most tragic among the literary and artistic visitors to Hastings were Dante Gabriel Rossetti and Elizabeth Siddal, the latter coming in search of a cure for the mysterious ailment which afflicted her. She is familiar to us through the languishing portraits which Rossetti painted, and also as the dead Ophelia in the well-known painting by Millais.

The romance between Dante Gabriel and 'Lizzie' Siddal, which had started so glowingly with Rossetti's adoration for the lovely girl of 17 with the mass of red-gold hair, was undeniably dimmed by the time of their Hastings stay; and Lizzie, after 10 years of indecisiveness on the part of the reluctant bridegroom, was disillusioned and ill. It is fairly certain that Rossetti believed he was marrying a dying woman

64. Old Hastings House, which stands at the point where High Street and All Saints Street merge. It was the home of the Victorian poet, Coventry Patmore.

when at last poor, ailing Lizzie was united with her brilliant but moody lover. The Cutter Inn, on the Old Town's seafront, incorporates in its structure No. 12 East Parade where Dante Gabriel stayed prior to their marriage in St. Clement's Church, Hastings, on 23 May 1860.

The sequel is gloomier still. They settled in London, and for a time health and happiness seemed to return. Then the birth of a still-born child was a grief too deep for this emotional pair to face. On 11 February 1862 Lizzie died from an overdose of laudanum, less than two years after they had stood at the altar together in St. Clement's Church, Hastings. Rossetti, distraught by grief and his conviction that neglect might have caused the tragedy, placed his unpublished poems

65. St. Clement's Church dates from 1390, when it was built to replace an earlier church destroyed in the French raid of 1377. Here Dante Gabriel Rossetti and Elizabeth Siddal were married on 23 May 1860.

in his wife's coffin; and so the grave in Highgate Cemetery closed over the remains of Elizabeth Siddal, the book of poems lying against the glory of her red-gold hair. But as the years passed, Rossetti's urge to retrieve the poems grew stronger and ever stronger, culminating in as grim a scene as it is possible to imagine. In the darkness of an October night in 1869 the coffin was dug up, opened, and the poems removed. They were to bring Rossetti poetic fame but little happiness.

Some of the most attractive groups of houses in the Old Town are clustered behind raised pavements in both High Street and All Saints Street, and one tiny half-timbered building bears the name Dickens Cottage, although the association seems obscure. An extraordinary erection is *The Piece of Cheese,* a house built on a wedge-shaped piece of land just off All Saints Street; it is, indeed, so narrow in shape that it looks exactly like a thriftily-thin piece of Cheddar cheese. Especially charming is the courtyard of houses entitled Sinnock Square, approached by an alleyway from High Street which is so unobtrusive that it is easily missed. This courtyard was once known as Tripe Alley, for it belonged to a butcher named Sinnock who sold tripe here.

A stroll up the steep road beside St. Clement's Church reveals more old houses in abundance whichever way you turn; and if you mount the steps close to All Saints Church, and wander along the whole length of Old Humphrey Avenue, you are walking in the footsteps of General Sir Arthur Wellesley, who lived in Hastings House, on this site, in the days before he became the great Duke of Wellington. It was to Hastings House that the future Iron Duke brought his bride in 1806, the year of William Pitt's death. Here, too, Lord Byron stayed during a visit to Hastings in 1814, and it is related that the hot-tempered poet flung an ink-bottle from one of the windows at the statue of the Muse of Lyric Poetry. Perhaps, like most writers and poets, he was suffering from one of those 'drying-up' patches when the pen comes to a stubborn halt, and the smugly inspired statue was more than he could bear. The house has now vanished. As far as 'Old Humphrey' himself is concerned, he was George Mogridge, a Victorian writer of children's stories who is largely forgotten today except for the avenue which bears his name.

At the Stag Inn in All Saints Street a somewhat chilling rarity awaits the visitor—a couple of fossilized cats hanging above the bar, hardly contributing to the general feeling of conviviality. They were found buried within the walls when repairs were being carried out early in the present century, and the poor, wretched creatures are thought to have been placed there as a protection against evil spirits. I was told at the inn

66. 'The Piece of Cheese' is a building in Hastings Old Town whose shape conforms very closely to its title.

that the age of these cats was believed to be about 400 years. The inn is older than it appears at a first glance, for the Georgian frontage masks a much earlier building.

Some good smugglers' tales are told of the Stag Inn, and it is said that at one time a hoard of both gold and brandy was found here. A secret tunnel exists from the cellars, and this climbs the hillside, passes beneath the road named Tackleway, and reaches its destination in a cave on the East Hill. The inn was known in earlier days as the White Hart, and the original bar was where the cellar is now located. Down in this cellar is the fireplace around which the occupants of the bar would gather, and beside it the tunnel starts. At its beginning is an opening, through which the smugglers could keep an eye on the occupants of the bar—just to be sure there was no excise-man there when they emerged. A diagram showing the route of the tunnel hangs on a wall of the ground-floor bar. Another favoured smugglers' inn was the Hastings Arms in George Street (see Chapter 7). Here troops were billeted during the Napoleonic Wars, and they were doubtless on good terms with the smugglers.

Before the creation of St. Leonards as a fashionable resort the landing of contraband on that part of the shore was frequent, and the great flat rock known as the Conqueror's Stone was a favourite landmark used by the smugglers for beaching their cargoes. The rather doubtful history of this stone is, firstly, that William the Conqueror used it as a table for a meal shortly after his landing at nearby Pevensey in 1066; and secondly, that it covered the spot on the seashore which formed King Harold's first temporary grave. Both stories are extremely legendary—but that the old stone witnessed the landing of many a cargo of illicit brandy and other delicacies is open to no doubt at all.

The principal churches of Hastings are of considerable interest and are very different in character. Apart from the ruins on Castle Hill, the two oldest are St. Clement's and All Saints, both having replaced earlier churches destroyed during the disastrous French raid of 1377. St. Clement's was rebuilt in 1390, but the French had not finished with it; towards the end of the seventeenth century a passing French warship

fired several cannonballs into the town and one lodged near
the top of St. Clement's sturdy tower. Here it remained, for
instead of removing it the citizens of Hastings placed another

67. **Sinnock Square** is a peaceful little courtyard-square behind the High Street
of Hastings Old Town. A butcher named Sinnock once sold tripe here, and the
square was, in fact, originally named Tripe Alley.

alongside, to complete the pattern! Today those two cannonballs are as firmly installed as ever. The church suffered again
in the Second World War (from the Germans this time), when
much damage was done by blast and the east windows were
destroyed.

There are two fine chandeliers in the nave, and the one nearest to the chancel is a Cinque Ports relic; it was the gift of the Barons of the Cinque Ports, and was made from a portion of the silver staves supporting the canopy at the coronation of King George III in 1761. It is easy to imagine how incensed those Barons would have been had they known the sequel— that when gaslight was installed in the church in 1836 the chandeliers were sold for a mere £5. This action was sadly characteristic of the nineteenth century, when so many valuable and historic church fittings throughout the whole country were given mediocre replacements. In 1923 the chandeliers were recovered and restored to the nave. Similar good fortune retrieved some shattered remnants of the rood screen which had been long lost, for in 1933, during the rebuilding of a house close to the church, parts of the screen were discovered in the building's structure. These consisted of a main beam which once spanned the nave or an aisle, the central arch lintel, and several pieces of arcading and uprights. They are now preserved within the church.

Close to the remains of the rood screen is a framed reproduction of the Bayeux tapestry, which provides an excellent opportunity to study this unique contemporary record of the Norman Conquest and the Battle of Hastings. This print (extracted from Arthur Mee's *Children's Encyclopaedia*) offers —as do so many publications intended for children—some marvellously concise information for adults. For instance, we learn that the tapestry was over 19 inches high and more than 200 feet long, that it portrayed 72 scenes with 623 men and women, 762 animals, 41 ships and 37 buildings. It was embroidered on linen and was not, therefore, a tapestry at all. After seeing this reproduction, I would suggest that the next step should be to study Hastings' modern version, for one of the most important features of the town's 1966 anniversary celebrations of the great battle of 1066 was the completion of another 'tapestry'. This, carried out by the Royal School of Needlework, brought the record of the country's history up to date from the Conquest to the present day. At the time of writing it is on view in the White Rock Pavilion, but there is a possibility that a permanent home will be provided for it so that it may always be on view to visitors to Hastings.

All Saints' Church was not rebuilt until 1436, 46 years later than St. Clement's. At one time its walls were completely covered with paintings, but today the Doom painting above the chancel arch alone survives. As a Cinque Port record this is a sad loss, for on the north wall sixteenth-century ships were depicted, with a sailor clad in the white coat with a red cross upon it which every Cinque Portsman was ordered to wear.

An interesting monumental brass of c. 1520 commemorates Thomas and Margaret Goodenough, who lie buried here. This is claimed to be the oldest surviving representation of a Bailiff of Hastings before this office was raised to the dignity of Mayor (by Charter of 1588). He is depicted on the brass opulently clad in a fur-trimmed robe. A simpler relic preserved in All Saints' Church is part of the old pump which earlier supplied water from the Bourne stream to the people of the parish; in view of the unsavoury state of the stream at this time one wonders how anyone reached a healthy old age at all.

A former Rector of All Saints was the Reverend Samuel Oates, father of the ignoble Titus Oates, whose fictitious 'Popish Plot' accusations of 1678 caused the death and imprisonment of large numbers of innocent people; he even attempted to implicate Charles II's Queen. Titus Oates was baptized in All Saints' Church in 1660, at the age of 11, and his subsequent record seems to have been that of the incurable delinquent. He was expelled from school, sent down from University, and then returned to Hastings where, of all unsuitable appointments, he was made Curate of All Saints. His behaviour in the church was so scandalous that on one occasion the congregation actually threw him out. When his fictitious Popish Plot was detected he was found guilty of false accusations and perjury, and in 1685 he suffered so severe a flogging in the pillory, followed by public exposure for three consecutive days, that his survival was a surprise to one and all. The house where he lived in Hastings is believed to have been on the Old London Road, just beyond Coventry Patmore's home, but no trace of it exists today.

The Church of St. Mary-in-the-Castle (on the sea-front, westwards from the Old Town) is especially notable for a curiosity—that within its walls is the spring which many centuries ago supplied water to the first St. Mary's (the Collegiate Church on Castle Hill) and to the soldiers of the castle. It forms the centre-piece of Pelham Crescent which, with its array of Regency balconies, was built in the 1820's and forms one of the most pleasing sections of the Hastings sea-front. The whole composition of the Crescent and church is, however, sadly obscured by the row of shops built in front.

Pelham Crescent and its church were built by the first Earl of Chichester in the 1820's, the church intended as a private family chapel. In 1884 it was presented to the parish by the third Earl, and on his death two years later its restoration was deemed a fitting memorial to a man who had devoted so much of his life to the affairs of the Church and of Sussex. He was for 50 years President of the Church Missionary Society and for 25 years Lord Lieutenant of Sussex. Nearly 100 years later the church was neglected and faced the risk of demolition, but when I visited it in May 1971 workmen were again busy, and St. Mary-in-the-Castle was coming to life again.

At a first glance the church forms an unexpectedly solid piece of classical architecture in the middle of the Regency balconies of Pelham Crescent. Its frontage consists of four very stolid Ionic columns crowned by a pediment, and inside it is a lofty circular building, with a colonnaded gallery above the central space. The whole design was dictated by the rock formation of the hill against which it stands, and this position is emphasized when one looks up to the gallery, for the rugged face of the rocky cliff peers in at the windows. This church, fully restored, could have an appeal of its own. Beyond the main body of the church is the old spring, and when St. Mary's is silent and empty you are led to it by the unrelenting drip-drip of the water, falling in inevitable drops since the days when St. Thomas Becket was Dean of the first St. Mary-in-the-Castle on the hilltop above.

Farther westwards, at St. Leonards, the parish church is new. Its predecessor received a direct hit from a flying bomb in 1944, and in its place has risen what is, to me, the most

impressive modern parish church that I have yet seen. So
many modern churches seem to reflect the atmosphere of a
conference hall rather than a place of worship, but the impression gained on entering this new church at St. Leonards
is immediately one of great dignity, beauty and devotion.
There is a story to be told about the church's rebirth after the
bombing, and this does, I think, go some way towards ex-
plaining the special sense of reverence within its walls.

The late Rector, Canon Cuthbert Griffiths, M.C., was at an
army cadet camp near Chichester on 29 July 1944 when the
news was brought to him that a direct hit had reduced his
church to a mass of rubble. The building had been shaken
plenty of times and its windows broken, but this time a
flying bomb came in under the trolley-bus wires and struck
the church, also demolishing the houses on either side. On the
following night the Rector had a dream, so forceful that it
governed all his future actions for the rebuilding of the church.
He dreamt that he was in the Holy Land, and there he beheld
Christ, preaching to the people from a boat on the Sea of
Galilee; and among the crowds listening were familiar faces
from his own parish—the old parish clerk, and a young
soldier (killed shortly afterwards) and his bride who were the
last couple to be married in the bombed church.

This dream gave birth to his determination to visit Galilee,
and to build the pulpit of the new church in the form of the
prow of the sacred ship. And when the present church,
designed by Adrian Gilbert Scott, reached completion in
1961, the wooden pulpit did take this form. It was made by
a Jewish carpenter on the shore of the Sea of Galilee, at the
foot of the hill of Gennesaret; the oak came from the forest of
Baashan, and it was seasoned by the age-old custom used since
the time of Christ—alternately, over a period of months,
soaking in the waters of Galilee and then drying out in the
hot Galilean sun.

The story of the pulpit is only part of the inspiration of this
church. It is the great semi-eliptical arches which achieve so
fine a sense of dignity, loftiness, proportion and veneration.

The other Hastings church which I want to mention is the
Fishermen's Church which stands among the net shops on the

foreshore of the Old Town. It is no longer used for its original purpose except for the services which take place on Sunday evenings in summer (from Whit Sunday until the Harvest Festival service in September). These are still primarily for the fishermen and seafarers, and it is a tradition that 'Eternal Father, strong to save', the hymn for those in peril on the sea, shall always be sung at the close of the service.

At other times this little foreshore church adopts its role as the Fishermen's Museum, dominated by the *Enterprise,* which occupies most of its space. This was the last of the old Hastings fishing luggers built for sail only at Rock-a-nore on the Old Town's foreshore, and it is a fine sight, with a model of a Hastings fisherman standing at the helm. His rugged, weather-beaten face, crowned by the traditional sou'wester hat, was modelled by the sculptress, Clare Sheridan, kinswoman of Sir Winston Churchill. Visitors to the museum can climb up on to the deck of the *Enterprise*—which, of course, children especially love to do—and here is the small portable pulpit used by the Rector of All Saints when he takes the service.

There is not room for a vast museum in this small Fishermen's Church, but all the exhibits are of interest. I found especially intriguing the stuffed albatross, for few of us have the opportunity to realize the size of this almost mythical bird of immense proportions. It can have a wing-span of 17 feet, and the specimen at Hastings has its wings fully extended; the head is turned sideways so that the beak, with its cruel hook, is well seen. No sailor will kill an albatross, for there is a strong seafaring superstition that on doing so his ship will sail to its doom. How this albatross came to be killed and stuffed is not related.

There are two major museums in Hastings—the Museum and Art Gallery at John's Place, off the Bohemia Road, and the Old Town Museum, housed in the Old Town Hall in the High Street. In the former there are exhibits relating to the old Sussex iron industry, pottery, old prints, and all sorts of items concerning Hastings, including a model of the Battle of Hastings. This shows the scene at noon on 14 October 1066, with the Saxons still holding the high ground, and Duke

William leading the cavalry with the aim of restoring the position after the Breton forces had retreated into marshy ground. There the unfortunate Bretons are seen, with their horses struggling as they sink into the bog. Compared with modern warfare it all seems incredibly small-scale for a battle that was to shape the future of this country from that time until the present day. Among the ceramics in the museum are some exceptionally good examples of the nineteenth-century Rye pottery of the hop and hop leaf design.

It is the Old Town Museum, however, that specially concerns the seeker after relics of Hastings as a Cinque Port, for here will be found some of the best examples of the 'Honours at Court' trophies, including parts of the canopies borne by the Barons at the coronations of Queen Anne, George III and George IV. The canopy held over Queen Anne was, for many years, used as an altar cloth in All Saints' Church. There are also fine examples of the robes of a Baron worn at the coronations of George III, George IV and Edward VII. Old prints depict the pageantry of these processions, and a wealth of Cinque Ports information is supplied beside each showcase.

Much Regency and Early Victorian architecture has been lost west of the Old Town owing to the dread hand of the demolisher and developer, but Wellington Square, at the foot of Castle Hill Road, is a charming Regency survival—only spoilt by the blank-faced modern building which closes the vista at the sea-front end.

In nearby Queen's Road is the Town Hall (a Victorian building for which even the most loyal Hastings citizen would not claim architectural distinction), and inside is something that affords constant surprise to Canadian visitors. It is the French coat of arms from the gates of Quebec. This is, in fact, a replica, for in the 1920's the original was returned to Quebec —whereupon that city sent Hastings the splendid replica which hangs in the Town Hall today, looking just as fine as the original.

Hastings' two Corporate Members in the Cinque Ports Confederation (after Winchelsea and Rye had acquired Head Port status) were Seaford and Pevensey.

Seaford was an important medieval town, with a good

harbour at the mouth of the River Ouse; but it suffered the same fate as Romney, for the river changed its course and the harbour silted up. It is now a seaside resort favoured by golfers.

Pevensey retains its place firmly entrenched in the pages of history as the landing-place of William the Conqueror—the last successful invasion of this country. It was also the location of one of the mighty Saxon Shore Forts of the Romans, and within the walls of this Roman Fort the Normans built their fortress. In medieval times it underwent several sieges, but by the date of the Spanish Armada (1588) its condition was so ruinous that, although equipped with a couple of cannon, it was considered of little importance. In 1940, however, the castle resumed its old role and became, yet again, a defence post against the threatened German invasion. With walls 12 feet thick, which rise to a great height, it is a magnificent sight.

But the historic landing-place has gone, for the sea has receded and left an inland scene where, on that fateful day in 1066, William of Normandy led his men ashore.

13. Sandwich

There is not even a glimpse of the sea at Sandwich today, yet this was in early times a mighty Cinque Port and the favoured place of arrival and departure of kings. Then the sea withdrew, and Sandwich was left two miles inland.

The height of the town's power, as a port and trading centre, was between the eleventh and thirteenth centuries, when Sandwich was the recognized English landing-place for travellers to London and for pilgrims to the shrine of St. Thomas Becket at Canterbury. This status as a port was owed primarily to Sandwich's harbour at the head of the Wantsum Channel, which at that time separated the Isle of Thanet from the mainland so that it was an isle in reality instead of in name alone, as it is today.

Before the birth of Sandwich as a port, or even as a place at all, the Romans had recognized the value of the sheltered Wantsum, and where the massive ruins of Richborough Castle now stand on the outskirts of the town the invasion army of the Emperor Claudius landed in A.D. 43. Here the Romans built their fort of Rutupiae (now Richborough) and this, with Reculver at the northern end of the Wantsum, guarded this important waterway. Richborough became the chief Roman supply base and administrative centre, and later it was outstanding among the string of Roman shore forts built to repel Saxon raiders. It was obvious, therefore, that another town and port would eventually occupy this position when the Romans left.

Before Sandwich appeared on the scene the ancient town of Stonar (opposite, across the Wantsum) had already come into being, and this remained a place of very considerable importance until it disappeared almost without trace in the fourteenth century. In 1365 it was practically submerged by the sea, and then the French burnt it to the ground in a raid exactly 20 years later. In Saxon times, however, Stonar prospered greatly, and by the seventh century Sandwich itself was coming into the picture as a port, for it is recorded that in c. 664–5 St. Wilfrid, returning from France shortly after his consecration to the episcopal see of York, came ashore 'happily and pleasantly in Sandwich Haven'.

In pre-Conquest times Sandwich was granted to the Priory of Christchurch in Canterbury. Then, in 1049, the town gained prominence when Edward the Confessor established his residence there, making the harbour a strategic base for his fleet— for this was a time of strife, with Danish raiders from across the sea and with the ambitious Earl Godwin (father of King Harold) at home. For long years Sandwich remained a possession of Christchurch, and at the time of the Domesday Book of 1086 was paying an annual rental of £40 to Canterbury, together with a yearly contribution of 40,000 herrings—almost as important, or more so, in those days. Not until the thirteenth century was this monastic ownership of Sandwich brought to an end, the first Mayor being elected in 1226.

From the time of the Conquest there is a constant record of great personages landing at Sandwich, or sailing from its harbour; and most celebrated of all these travellers in the eyes of posterity was St. Thomas Becket. Following his stormy meeting with King Henry II at the Council of Northampton in 1164 he sailed from Sandwich, in great secrecy, to exile in France. First of all, however, he sought refuge in Eastry, his Manor about two miles to the south-west of Sandwich. In some descriptions of St. Thomas's flight the impression is gained that he left the castle at Northampton and sailed for France that very night; but early chronicles indicate that this was not so, and in the church guide at Eastry are quoted two accounts which are considered to be the most reliable on St. Thomas Becket's period of refuge there. They are of great interest and therefore I will quote them:

'Now inasmuch as he standeth in need both of men and horses and craft wherein to cross south overseas, but is himself no longer well furnished with money, he wendeth towards a certain sea town called Eastry, over which there ruleth a certain Prior who oweth allegiance to Canterbury.

The archbishop therefore maketh himself and all his will clearly known unto him. He came here some days before the mass of All Saints, and tarieth over the feast. He standeth in a little side chapel while mass is being sung and seeth from there the body of the Lord. The Prior findeth him a little boat for his sea faring, and two brisk mass-brothers to make him fellowship. This time the mass of All Saints fell on a Monday, and the night next following it a good hour before day break, the holy Thomas goeth from Eastry forth upon the sea with his three bretheren and putteth to sea away from England at the place called Sandwich, and the third day, Tuesday that he is on the sea is the fifteenth from the Tuesday when he was so hard afflicted at Northampton.' (From *Thomas Saga Erkibyskups*—Magnusson—thought to be based on the lost Chronicle of Robert of Cricklade.)

The second account is from the Chronicle of Allan of Tewkesbury:

'At length coming to Eastry, a manor of the Prior of Christ Church, Canterbury, there for some days he waited in concealment, where an orifice having been made in a wall, for he was close to the church, he heard masses with the people. Even the priest who was celebrating did not know of his presence. A clerk who knew the secret brought him the kiss of peace. And when the people returned after the service, Becket bestowed his episcopal blessing on them although they were unaware of it.'

So St. Thomas Becket, together with the 'brisk mass-brothers', sailed away from Sandwich in a craft that seems perilously small if the portrayal in Queen Mary's Psalter in the British Museum is anything to go by. Six years later he returned, reaching Sandwich harbour on 1 December 1170, and here crowds gave him a joyous welcome, which was repeated all the way along his route to Canterbury. But the hours of St. Thomas's life were running out, and three days after Christmas the four knights met at Saltwood Castle to complete their murderous plans for the following day.

The next historic landing at Sandwich Haven was in 1194

when Richard I, Coeur de Lion, stepped ashore on his return from the Crusades and imprisonment in Austria. (He had been seized during his journey back from the Holy Land and held captive by the Emperor Henry VI from 1192 to 1194.) On payment of a heavy ransom he was released, and it was to give thanks for his eventual safe return that Richard I made his way in pilgrimage from Sandwich to Canterbury Cathedral.

Another of history's most colourful royal personages, Edward the Black Prince, landed at Sandwich in 1357. This followed his great victory at Poitiers in the previous year, and he brought with him, as royal prisoner, King John of France.

Exactly a century later, in 1457, a very different French landing took place. In that year a force of 4,000 men from Honfleur, under the command of Marshal de Brézé, came ashore and not only pillaged the town but murdered the Mayor, John Drury. To this day the Mayor of Sandwich wears a black robe in mourning for this deed, and black bows ornament his chain of office. Deal, as a Corporate Member of Sandwich, also adopts a black robe, but with gold trimmings to indicate half-mourning; all other Mayors of the Cinque Ports are clad in red. It is good to know that, despite the black mourning robe of the Mayor, Sandwich and Honfleur have long been on the best of terms and, since 1958, have been twin towns exchanging regular visits of their citizens.

By the beginning of the sixteenth century the Port had declined in importance, for silting-up was in progress and the sea was receding. The whole of the sixteenth century was, for Sandwich, a record of struggle to save the harbour and of appeals to the Crown for help. Henry VIII was petitioned in the early 1530's for aid, and the King did show his concern by making a personal visit to the town, when he was conducted to the Thanet side of the Wantsum in order better to survey the situation. The King offered help for reconstruction of the harbour—but this characteristically took the form of granting funds raised from the sale of all the precious jewels, ornaments and plate in the possession of Sandwich's three parish churches.

Henry VIII again visited Sandwich for a couple of days in 1539, but he was then engaged, with great urgency, in building his series of defensive castles and forts along the coast. It was at this time that the Tudor Barbican was built as a blockhouse, and it still stands picturesquely at the toll-bridge (Thanet road) entrance to the town.

No permanent benefit resulted from enlisting Henry VIII's aid, and therefore, early in the reign of Queen Elizabeth I, a further petition was made for Crown assistance in restoring the haven; and when the Queen visited the town in 1573 there were high hopes that aid would result.

For this great occasion the houses and streets were made gay with decorations, and the gilded heraldic beasts still preserved in the Guildhall were part of the ornamentation of the Sandown Gate, through which the Queen entered the town. Here she was met by the Mayor wearing a scarlet robe—believed to be the only time, since the murder of John Drury, that his black robe has been abandoned; but the Queen forbade this sombre apparel, saying she would have no mourning when she came to the town. As she stood for the traditional handing over of the town mace, guns were fired, muskets discharged, and drums beaten in royal salute—all with such precision that the Queen was highly impressed. She then progressed through the streets of Sandwich, orations were made, and a fine golden cup was presented to her.

The town was in truly festive mood, as was the Queen, and the celebrations were on a grand scale. Entertainment during her three-day visit included a mock battle in the harbour, and, to liven up one of the intervals, two Walloon citizens sailed their boats to a head-on collision at such speed that the loser was thrown into the water—'at which the Queen had good sport' says the record.

The third day of the visit was marked by a grand banquet in the grounds of Sir Roger Manwood's School, prepared by the wives of the Mayor and Jurats and consisting of 160 different dishes. The Queen could not sample them all, though she tasted many and ignored the customary safe-guards against poison. With kindly diplomacy she insisted on several of the untasted delicacies being carried away to her lodging so that she might enjoy them later. The banquet was a splendid success and the Queen was 'very merrye'.

But nothing emerged from the royal visit to aid 'amendment of the Haven', and as the years went by deterioration continued apace. Queen Elizabeth I's visit was always remembered warmly, however, in Sandwich. Not so the visit of Queen Catherine of Braganza in 1672. She came with King Charles II and the Duke of York (the latter Lord Warden of the Cinque Ports and later King James II). The Queen refused to emerge from her carriage and did not even place a foot upon the soil of Sandwich; in fact, a royal banquet had to be served at the Mayor's door so that she could partake of it in her coach.

Queen Elizabeth I showed much concern for the well-being of the Protestants from France and the Netherlands who sought refuge in this area, and although at first there were doubts among the English population at so great an influx of foreigners, these newcomers proved valuable to the future of Sandwich. They introduced fresh skills and trades, and the gabled architecture of Flemish origin is still prominent in some of the old houses of the town. Among the activities introduced by the Protestant refugees were market gardening and the production of serge, baize and flannel; and the nature of the town changed from a decaying port to a thriving market town.

Strangely enough it was the sea which, in its desertion of Sandwich, contributed finally to the town's prosperity, for the sandy soil left in its wake proved superbly suited to the game of golf. So the links came into being which are among the finest in the world (second only, in Britain, to the Royal and Ancient at St. Andrews) and at the Royal St. George's the oldest English golf competition is played, the St. George's Champion Grand Challenge Cup. Other famous courses are the Prince's at Sandwich, and the Royal Cinque Ports at nearby Deal.

Sandwich today has retained, without any symptom of 'quaintness' or self-consciousness, a quite remarkable legacy of its old character, customs and architecture. The streets are twisting, charming, and unspoilt—but I would suggest leaving the streets alone at the outset of a visit and setting out to gain an initial impression of this inland Cinque Port from the path which leads along the top of the old town ramparts.

68. The Barbican provides the entrance to Sandwich from the Thanet road and was built by Henry VIII in 1539 as part of his fortification of the coast against the invasion threat from the Continent.

These defensive walls are now represented by grass-grown slopes, very steep in places, which lead down to where the encircling moat once flowed. It is possible to make an almost complete tour of the town along this route of the walls, the only break being encountered near the Barbican gateway, where it is necessary to turn aside and walk along Strand Street.

The various stretches of the ramparts bear different names. From the end of Strand Street, where the old Canterbury Gate originally stood, the path leads past the Recreation Ground—outside the walls, and in the old days this was the Plague

H

69. The old ramparts of Sandwich. It is possible to walk round most of Sandwich by the pathway which leads along the top of the grass-grown ramparts of the old town.

Field where all who were afflicted were isolated and buried. Then, after passing the back of the Tannery, the section of the rampart walk known as the Butts is reached, a length of greensward which earned its title because this is where archery was practised; it is believed that some of Henry v's archers, who contributed so valiantly to the victory at Agincourt, perfected their skill here.

After the Butts a road is crossed at the site of the old

70. **The Fisher Gate** was in earlier times the water gate entrance to the walled town of Sandwich for travellers arriving from the Isle of Thanet.

Woodnesborough Gate, and then the Rope Walk is embarked upon. From here the best view is gained (if the foliage of the trees is not too dense) of the garden side of the White Friars, the home of Sandwich's celebrated eighteenth-century historian, William Boys; the attractive Flemish gables of the house are well seen from this aspect, for these do not appear on the frontage in New Street. The name, White Friars, derives from a monastic house of the Carmelites founded on this site in 1272 and dissolved during the reign of Henry VIII. Beside the Rope Walk is the Town Ditch, and the path is pleasantly shaded in summer by an avenue of limes.

The next section of the ramparts is Mill Wall, which leads to the site of the vanished Sandown Gate, through which Queen Elizabeth I entered the town on the festive occasion of her visit in 1573. Then the Bulwark is reached, with the picturesque Fisher Gate beside the River Stour; this was the watergate entrance from the Isle of Thanet, and its lower portion dates from the fourteenth century, the rest from the sixteenth century, the decade prior to Queen Elizabeth's visit. Behind the Fisher Gate is the fine old Customs House.

After the rampart walk the Guildhall is the next place to visit, for here a good deal can be learned about the background of Sandwich which will make exploration of the town all the more interesting. Here too, is the Museum, which I shall describe towards the end of this chapter.

The modern exterior of the Guildhall provides a disappointing first impression, but inside it presents a very different picture for the Council Chamber, Mayor's Parlour and most of the Court Room are survivals from the sixteenth century. On clanging the bell by the side entrance, you can enlist the aid of the Town Sergeant in showing all the Guildhall's fascinating contents. But should misfortune strike, in the form of the Town Sergeant's absence or a meeting in progress which prevents touring the building, then try again later, for the Guildhall should not be missed.

In the Court Room is a stalwart wooden screen of about 1300 which has been retained from the medieval Guildhall, and on its two gateposts are the gilded heraldic beasts which decorated the Sandown Gate for Queen Elizabeth I's visit. The scene is depicted in the Court Room's stained glass window, where the Mayor and Jurats are seen receiving the Queen—the Mayor clad in scarlet as she desired. In this window are also depicted the halberds which now hang from the Court Room ceiling; they originally belonged to the

Cinque Ports Fleet and were later carried before Judges to the Assizes.

In the Guildhall there are two Cinque Ports relics: the original Royal Charter granted by King Charles II, and a

71. **The Customs House,** linked with the Fisher Gate by Quay Lane, is a reminder of the days before the sea receded from Sandwich. It is now a private residence.

quarter of the canopy borne by the Barons of the Cinque Ports at the coronation of King George III in 1761. Both are in superb condition and beautifully displayed. On one of the walls hangs the thirteenth-century Common Horn which was used for all royal proclamations and for summoning together the Freemen of the Port.

The Mayor's chair, in the Council Chamber, was made in 1561 and must be one of the finest of its kind in Britain; with its elaborately-carved armrests, it is a marvellous piece of craftsmanship. Behind hang a series of four paintings of

Author's photograph, reproduced by courtesy of the Sandwich Corporation.

72. The Mayor's Chair in the Council Chamber of Sandwich's Guildhall. The elaborately carved arms bear the date 1561.

historical rather than artistic merit, but well worth studying. They portray the visit to Sandwich, on 4 May 1672, of Charles II, Queen Catherine of Braganza, and the Lord Warden of the Cinque Ports, the future James II. The Canterbury Gate (no longer in existence) is depicted, and the Queen is seen installed in the carriage which she so stubbornly refused to leave.

At the Guildhall are kept the three Sandwich maces—two small maces of the fifteenth century and a larger one dating from George I's reign. It was the larger of the two small maces which was presented to Queen Elizabeth I on her famous visit. When showing these to me, the Town Sergeant gave me some enlightening details about maces in general. Should the Monarch or Mayor be attacked in the old days, the mace was to be used for clubbing the assailant, and the Town Sergeant was the person to wield it. From early times up to the present day the mace has played an important part in ceremonial, and on any royal visit the Monarch is received either at the gateway of the town or at the Guildhall or Town Hall, where the Mace Bearer (in the case of the Confederation of the Cinque Ports, always the Town Sergeant) waits with the mace on his right shoulder. As soon as the Monarch's foot is placed on the soil or pavement, the mace is turned upside down with the bowl in the Town Sergeant's hand as a symbol that the Sovereign is now in charge of the borough.

In Sandwich there is an interesting old custom in the form of the Mayor's Wand of Office. This consists of a tall, thin and very straight blackthorn stick which is carried by the Mayor on every civic occasion. Its purpose, when the custom began, is said to have been to protect the Mayor against witches. A fresh blackthorn stick is produced each year for the new Mayor and to prepare this the Town Sergeant goes out into the countryside each October (when the sap is down in the bushes) and searches the hedgerows for a good new blackthorn stick. He cuts and straightens it—the method of straightening being to soak the stick until pliable and then to tie it to a broomstick (most appropriate treatment for this anti-witch weapon!). The stick is then dried out in the Guildhall boiler-house. Finally, when beautifully straight and firm, the Town Sergeant paints it with black lacquer and it is ready for presentation at the Mayormaking in May.

When the Mayormaking day arrives the Town Sergeant, with due ceremony, presents the Mayor with the new Wand of Office, and in exchange the Mayor gives him a coin to the value of a crown. These coins are sometimes of very considerable value; for instance, the 1971 crown was a William III of 1696. Each Mayor keeps his blackthorn stick at the end of his term of office—and with all these ex-Mayors around the witches of Sandwich must have a thin time.

On quite a number of days in the year the Mayor and Corporation walk in procession through the town in full regalia, the route being from the Guildhall to St. Clement's Church. These occasions include Mayor's Sunday (the first

Sunday after the Mayormaking in May), Battle of Britain Sunday, Remembrance Sunday, Sir Roger Manwood's Founder's Day, and the Confirming of the Deputies (in July). The last-named is the day when the men who are sworn in as Mayor Deputy of each Member town come to Sandwich to pay their Ship Money—still contributed at the traditional rates of long ago. Taking examples, Brightlingsea pays 10 silver shilling pieces, Fordwich the sum of 3s. 4d., but Sarre, for some reason which I have not grasped, has not paid anything for about 400 years. The Deputies are ceremonially handed their chains of office, among which the Brightlingsea chain is especially fine—composed of crossed silver fishes and silver oyster shells, with a medallion containing one of the largest opals in the world. Sarre (since this Member town is 3s. 4d. better off than Fordwich) does not qualify for a chain of office at all, but receives instead a stave of office. The Ship Money is now, of course, paid in the decimal equivalent.

Another old custom which has survived in Sandwich is the ringing of the curfew, and this still peels nightly, at eight p.m., from St. Peter's Church. In the old days the sound of the curfew meant that all had to dowse their fires and turn their hogs and geese out into the streets (the idea apparently being that they ate up the refuse during the night). At 5 a.m. the goose bell used to be rung, and the man of the house had to secure his hogs and geese and put them into their own pens. Failing to do this meant that the Town Sergeant and 15 helpers would round up all the hogs and geese and take them to St. Bartholomew's Hospital. In other words, the owners lost their meat and eggs for the year.

On 24 August each year Sandwich celebrates 'St. Barts. Day' when the new Master of St. Bartholomew's Hospital is 'pricked out' by the Chairman of the Trustees. This takes place in the Chapel, and from the list of the men of the alms-houses the Master is literally chosen by pricking his name with a bodkin. After this little ceremony the Mayor and Trustees file out into the courtyard where the children of Sandwich take part in a race for the 'Bartlemas Bun'. For this they have to run round the chapel and the winner gets a St. Barts Biscuit; the rest get sticky buns. If the winner is hungry that is just too

73. **The Norman tower of St. Clement's Church** is a magnificent sight and a notable Sandwich landmark. The tower dates from about 1100.

bad, for the biscuit is so hard that it is quite inedible. In fact, the St. Barts Biscuit is regarded as a trophy, to be kept—but there is a good chance that the child who wins will get a sticky bun as well.

Among the churches of Sandwich St. Clement's reigns supreme, and its superb Norman tower (c. 1100) surveys the town with massive dignity. Inside, an unusual heritage of the early architectural history of the church can be seen above the chancel arch, for here are still visible traces of the outline of the original Norman roof, while above can be detected the pointed outline of the next, Early English roof. The roof we see today, with its ornamentation of angels bearing shields, is of the fifteenth century. The octagonal font (believed to date from the beginning of the fifteenth century) has a rare feature in bearing the arms of the Cinque Ports on one of its heraldic shields.

There has been very considerable restoration in the church, but its antiquarian interest is nevertheless great. St. Margaret's Chapel, in the north aisle, retains its flooring of medieval tiles, and the altar consists of a medieval altar slab which had (at

74. **Traces of earlier roofs are visible** above the chancel arch in St. Clement's Church, Sandwich. The lowest line is that of the Norman roof, while above is the outline of the next Early English roof.

the time of the Reformation) been relegated for use as a pavement slab. The stone slab of the high altar suffered the same fate; for 350 years it served as a gravestone but is now restored to its original use. In the north aisle, above the doorway leading to the tower stairway, is a fine carved tympanum of either late Saxon or early Norman date.

A very unusual feature survives in the Chancel. At the foot of the choir stalls are round holes cut in the stone which correspond to orifices in the Sanctuary walls; these were, it seems, an early method of amplification and are regarded as a great rarity. Among the treasures of the church is a ciborium of c. 1510; this—which originally belonged to St. Mary's—in some mysterious way escaped Henry VIII's decision that all such items should be sold in aid of 'amendment of the haven'. There is also a later Elizabethan chalice, obviously provided to make good the losses caused by Henry VIII's generous allocation.

75. **This carved tympanum** above the tower stairway door of St. Clement's Church is attributed to the late Saxon or early Norman period.

Especially beautiful in St. Clement's (in my eyes, at any rate) is the figure of St. John which stands unobtrusively in a niche of the Chapel of St. George in the south aisle. This is believed to have come originally from Lincoln Cathedral, removed at the time of the Reformation, and the gentleness of the expression seems to express foregiveness for all past vicissitudes. When I was last in St. Clement's a church helper, dusting and polishing with admirable enthusiasm, seemed surprised at the veneration with which I gazed at the statue. 'Don't care much for these old things,' she said. 'The present's good enough for me.' And with a whack of her duster she departed. St. John continued to gaze downwards with gentle understanding. Worse things had happened to him, and he was, at least, being dusted.

St. Peter's Church, from which the curfew rings and where Thomas Paine, author of *The Rights of Man*, was married, has a square tower topped by a fanciful cupola which is almost as familiar a landmark of Sandwich as the great tower of St. Clement's. It can be seen tipping up above the roofs in almost every photograph or old print of the Tudor Barbican. This church has, however, suffered many disasters, and at the time

76. **Statue of St. John** in St. Clement's Church. This is believed to have had its origin in Lincoln Cathedral and to have been removed at the time of the Reformation.

of writing it is closed to the general public owing to the perilous condition of part of the roof.

Despite its present state of dilapidation, there is an impressive sense of dignity about St. Peter's. It was built during the stormy reign of King John, and its rather mystifying shape today is due to widening of the aisles in the fourteenth century and the loss of the south aisle in 1661 when the tower collapsed upon it, leaving it a total ruin. The position of this aisle, now grass-grown, can be recognized immediately by the curious little building, with Dutch gables, which stands at its east end. There are all sorts of suggestions about the uses to which this small building was put, including the inevitable possibility that at some time it served as a hiding-place for smuggled goods.

Among the rather battered memorials of St. Peter's is the effigyless tomb of Thomas Ellis, or Ellys, Mayor of Sandwich in 1370 and 1382. The canopied recess is damaged but far better left as it is than over-restored. Nearby, a less elaborate tomb niche still retains the effigies of John Ellis and his wife (c. 1360–1390). Another effigy is that of a knight in chain mail which has been attributed to Sir John Grove, 1450, but possibly dates from an earlier period. The knight is sadly damaged, his nose flattened, his legs gone from the knees; as a final indignity, in removal from the ruined south aisle to a safer position against the west wall the effigy was placed in reverse. So now the unfortunate knight, legless and noseless, faces resolutely to the west, the back of his head towards the altar. Perhaps one day this may be put right so that he can face the altar once more.

St. Mary's Church in Strand Street is of great antiquity. It is a great, bare and impressive church which was saved from demolition in 1956 only by concerted action on the part of the Friends of St. Mary's. The French did great damage to it in the fourteenth century, and in 1578 an earthquake shook the foundations so severely that this is thought to have contributed towards the collapse of the tower a century later. In falling it crashed on to the nave, with disastrous effect. Only the bases of the Norman columns now remain, some of them covered by protective boards (which can be lifted).

77. **Medieval Peter's Pence Box** in St. Mary's Church, Sandwich. This was used for collection of the Papal Tribute.

The font dates from Tudor times, and near it is a medieval Peter's Pence Box, used for the collection of the Papal Tribute. This offering, which originated in the time of King Offa of

Mercia as a voluntary contribution, developed into an ecclesiastical tax, frequently misused, and the cause of much ill-feeling; it was finally abolished, as might be expected, by Henry VIII. This Peter's Pence Box in St. Mary's is a very rare survival.

In the south-west corner of the church a number of Benefaction Boards line the wall, starting with the £11 annuity of Solomon Hougham in 1696 and ending with the 1956 benefaction. The latter states that the church had fallen into such disrepair that its demolition was sought—a calamity which was averted by the formation, under the chairmanship of the Mayor, of the Association of the Friends of St. Mary's. They raised a sum of £7,000 for repair of the fabric and for purchase of securities to be held in trust for the maintenance of the church in future years. A marvellous achievement, for the demolition of St. Mary's would have been tragic.

A few steps from the Guildhall is the Congregational Church, which also has claims to distinction, for it was one of the early examples of an independent chapel. It is simply designed, with a most pleasing sense of friendliness inside; a children's corner is equipped with small-sized chairs where the children sit during the services. Of special interest historically are the two central pillars made from ships' masts—the original masts of the ships in which French Protestant refugees arrived in this country and later presented to the church as a token of gratitude.

The town is full of attractive old houses, but the two most notable and picturesque are gabled Manwood Court and the half-timbered King's Lodging. It was traditionally from a bow-window of the King's Lodging that Queen Elizabeth viewed the fleet in 1573, for at that time the house overlooked the harbour. Manwood Court is where she was entertained with so many delicacies that she could not taste them all. In the garden is the copper beech which she is said to have planted on this grand occasion. Manwood Court was then, of course, one house; now it is divided between Manwood Court and Manwood Close, but to the general eye it is still an unspoilt whole. The date of construction, 1564, is on its front wall—it was therefore a grand and newly-built house when Queen

Elizabeth was entertained there. In this house the well-known Sir Roger Manwood's Grammar School had its premises from 1564 until 1858; the school is now located at the other end of the town, in Manwood Road, near Mill Wall.

On the opposite side of the road from Manwood Court is a remnant of the original stone section of the old town wall (behind a modern wall which fronts the road). A little farther on will be found the Guestling Stream and Gallows Field, situated just beyond the site of the old Canterbury Gate. Grisly old-time stories are told of this area, for in the Guestling Stream were drowned the witches of the town, and at high tide the Town Sergeant would open the sluice gates to let them out into the sea. After this treatment it seems strange that the Mayor should need a blackthorn stick to ward them off—but perhaps it was their avenging spirits that were after him. Gallows Field, so the story goes, is where criminals were buried alive. How serious their crime had to be for this drastic sentence I do not know—probably quite slight. Near by (as I mentioned earlier) was the Plague Field. This was not the most salubrious part of Sandwich in the old days —but all these places, the Guestling Stream, Gallows Field and the Plague Field, were outside the walls.

Back in the centre of the town there are two houses which I should mention. One is the Dutch House in King Street, a white building with distinctive Flemish ornamentation; as can be guessed, this was built by one of the many Flemish refugees who settled in Sandwich during the sixteenth century. The other is at 20 New Street, marked with a notice 'Tom Paine lived here, 1759'. The author of *The Rights of Man* was born at Thetford and died in New York, and his period in Sandwich was short. He began his working life as an apprentice to a staymaker (enough to foster revolutionary thoughts in any man) and it was in order to set up in his own business that he came to the Cinque Port of Sandwich. There he met and married Mary Lambert. But he did not prosper in the town, so they moved to Margate and in 1760 she died in childbirth. One short year had brought to Tom Paine failure in his work and the death of his wife. He little knew then that he would be well known to posterity.

78. **Dutch House** in King Street is an example of Sandwich's architectural inheritance from the Protestant refugees who fled from the Netherlands and settled in the town in the sixteenth century.

Visitors to Sandwich are often mystified by the name of a narrow alleyway which bears the title of Holy Ghost Alley. The origin is that the ancient half-timbered building opposite was once the town jail, and the prisoners' chapel was on the other side of the road; thus, Holy Ghost Alley was so named because the chapel was next door to it. When the prisoners had to work on the treadmill on the ramparts, they had to pass along this alleyway in single file, then through St. Clement's Churchyard, to reach the treadmill.

The Sandwich Museum housed in the Guildhall is full of interest, and whether it should be visited before or after exploring the town is a matter of choice. I always find local museums especially appealing *after* getting to know the town a little.

One of the items which I like best in this museum is the showcase where a selection of the town records is displayed. This is changed every three months, so that if it is possible to make quarterly visits the most fascinating bits of information about Sandwich's past reveal themselves. The 1971 summer selection included a record which struck a topical note. It read: 'Dissatisfaction with the Postal Service, 1662. The Corporation notes the great inconvenience caused by the lack of a weekly post to return money and goods to and from London. They wish to continue their own postal service, despite the recent Act of Parliament for erecting the Post Office.'

A letter of 1642, among these records, is unusual in its content. We are so accustomed to hearing of the destruction and misdeeds of the Cromwellian soldiers during the Civil War that it is revealing to come upon this letter, with its warning against the behaviour of the Royalist army. Apparently the King's 'outrageous Cavaleers' had much to answer for, and the writer warns the Mayor and Jurats that the King's forces have left destruction wherever they stayed and had 'ript up fetherbeds and thrown the fethers in the wind . . . and staved all the Barrels of beer and wine and spilt it . . . they have killed one man's 1,000 shepe and thrown away such of it as they could not eat.' There is little doubt which side Thomas Hilden, the writer of the letter, supported.

Royalist sentiments are later made clear in the records (not, however, on view in the museum at the same time as Thomas Hilden's letter), and the horror of the town is expressed at the execution of the King: 'This year was the Bloodyest year that ever came to poor England, for Cromwell and many more of that Cursed Limms of the Devil and firebrands of Hell consulted together, and upon the 30 day of January Most Wickedly

79. Holy Ghost Alley. In the old days the town jail was opposite, and the prisoners' chapel was adjacent to this curiously-named alleyway. This was the route the prisoners would take to work on the treadmill.

and most Traiterously Murdered our Gratious King Charles
the First so that we may cry out and say the Breath of our
Nostrill's the Lord's anointed was Taken in their pitt.'

All sorts of bygones are on view in the museum—including
two particularly unpleasant items from the Old Town Jail.
One is a sinister branding iron for the back, after which the
luckless sufferer would carry the words 'Sandwich House of
Correction' on his back for the rest of his life; another is a
smaller branding iron, with the same message destined for the
forehead. There are also some interesting items relating to the
sister town of Sandwich, in Illinois, U.S.A. The main Cinque
Ports items, the canopy and the Charter of Charles II, are not
in the museum for they are prominently displayed in the main
section of the Guildhall.

Outside Sandwich is Richborough Castle, approached by a
lane from the Canterbury road, and this is a phenomenal
survival of the Roman occupation. Now battered and broken,
its vast proportions are conveyed by the great stretches of
wall, immensely thick and strong, which still stand. Outside
the walls and within are a series of deep, grass-grown ditches.

Here landed the Claudian invasion forces commanded by
Aulus Plautius in A.D. 43. The use of the site was purely
practical in this early period of the Roman occupation,
serving first of all as the main base of the invasion forces and
then as a supply base. Towards the end of the century, however, when the conquest of Britain was considered final and
complete, Rutupiae was given a more splendid appearance; all
temporary wooden structures were demolished and an imposing central building was erected, composed of marble
and adorned with statues. Two centuries later Richborough
(or rather, Rutupiae) resumed its military character and, as
one of the Saxon Shore Forts of outstanding importance,
acquired the great outer walls which still survive, though
ruined, today.

There is an excellent plan near the entrance to Richborough
Castle which aids most admirably a mental reconstruction of
the great fort as one wanders around, and in the museum are
gathered together the archaeological finds that have been
made. It is an amazing sight, this great Roman castle of

80. **Richborough Castle,** on the outskirts of Sandwich, was the Rutupiae of the Romans and the landing-place of the Claudian invasion of A.D. 43. Of this great Roman fortress ruined walls survive of immense thickness and deep, grass-grown ditches. A museum displays archaeological finds.

Richborough, and at the end of the day, silent and empty, it does convey a strange sense of past echoes lingering on.

Another place that should not be missed in the neighbourhood of Sandwich is Eastry. There was a palace of the Kings of Kent here as early as the seventh century, and legend tells that this, and the Manor of Eastry, passed to the Priory of Christchurch in Canterbury as penance for a royal murder which took place within the palace walls. The site of this ancient palace is believed to be occupied by Eastry Court, close beside the church. But it is as the hiding-place of St. Thomas Becket that Eastry figures most prominently in the pages of history.

The Church of St. Mary the Virgin dates from the early thirteenth century; therefore it succeeded the Norman church where St. Thomas 'tarieth over the feast'. There is today no trace of the little side chapel where he stood, and where a hole in the wall enabled him to share in the celebration of mass without being observed. The church is, however, early enough to have inherited the Norman sense of massive solidarity in its structure, and its beauty is very striking as you open the door and step down into the great nave, with its fine arches and light flowing in from the clerestory above.

Over the chancel arch are four rows of medallion frescoes which date from the early thirteenth century and are, as the church guide explains, characteristic of the painted ornamentation which sometimes took the place of the cloth or tapestry hangings which enriched the rood in wealthier churches. Among the subjects depicted on the medallions are: a pair of doves, thought to represent the Holy Spirit and the Christian Soul; the lion, symbol of the Resurrection; the wyvern or dragon as a symbol of evil conquered by the Resurrection; and in the centre of all is a trefoil flower, possibly representing the Rod of Aaron.

Another feature of considerable rarity (which remains unnoticed except by those who know where to look for it) is the fourteenth-century perpetual calendar known as the Dominican Circle; it is on the south-west face of the only octagonal pillar (erected in 1327 to replace one of the circular pillars).

The tombs and monuments commemorate three important Eastry familes—the Nevinsons of Eastry Court; the Bargraves who, in the seventeenth century, succeeded the Nevinsons in ownership of Eastry Court; and the Botelers who came to Eastry at the end of the fourteenth century. For anyone who has delved into the history of Kent it is of interest to know that it was William Boteler of Eastry (d. 1818) who supplied Hasted with a great deal of the material on this part of the county for his *History and Topographical Survey of the County of Kent* (1797–1801).

In a glass case in the north aisle is a copy of the Vinegar Bible of 1717, so named owing to an error made by the printer, John Baskett; in this version the heading to the

Gospel of St. Luke, Chapter XX, reads 'The Parable of the Vinegar' instead of 'The Parable of the Vineyard'.

This is a really beautiful church and it is made all the lovelier by the sheer lavishness and care of the flower decorations, whose perfume greeted me as I opened the door.

Of Sandwich's Member towns, Deal and Walmer—who in earlier times were not even Corporate Members—have so soared in importance that they occupy the next chapter to themselves. Ramsgate, unlike its Head Port, remains a coastal town, and has become a popular seaside resort with a colourful harbour, gay with yachts and fishing-boats in summer. During the Second World War it was one of the major bases for the Dunkirk evacuation of 1940. Architecturally, Ramsgate has some fine crescents whose names indicate their period—the Wellington, Nelson and Royal Crescents, and the Paragon. At Pegwell Bay, which is almost an extension of Ramsgate, there is a thriving cross-Channel hoverport. Here was the traditional landing-place of Hengist and Horsa in A.D. 449; and half a mile inland—at a spot marked by a cross, from which the sea has long since receded—is Ebbsfleet, where St. Augustine came ashore in A.D. 597.

Brightlingsea, in Essex, is the only place in the whole list of the Confederation's Head Ports and their Member Towns which is not located in Kent or Sussex. It is still very maritime in character; far from being stranded inland like its Head Port, its life is dominated by the Brightlingsea Reach of the river Colne estuary and the creeks which flow eastwards from it. It has a long-standing reputation for yacht building, fishing and oysters—as may be gathered from the design of its Deputy's chain of office.

Sarre is a small inland place far more widely known for its cherry brandy than for maritime exploits; and Stonar, so important a town in the days of the medieval charters, has vanished altogether beneath the joint onslaughts of the sea and the French.

Fordwich was, in the heyday of the Confederation, the sole Corporate Member of Sandwich. Then, with the river Stour much wider than it is today, it was the port for Canterbury, with a harbour busy with medieval shipping. But the river

81. St. Thomas Becket sails from Sandwich into exile—as portrayed in the early fourteenth-century Queen Mary's Psalter in the British Museum. The Psalter was acquired by Queen Mary I in 1553 and for this reason bears her name.

shrank in size and Fordwich shrank in importance—though not in charm. Today it is an altogether delightful small riverside village, with a tiny half-timbered Town Hall and the fine Church of St. Mary the Virgin. Within the church is the ancient Fordwich Stone, a magnificent relic with carved interlaced arches and a sloping top of fish-scale design. Known popularly as St. Augustine's tomb, its origin is a mystery; the date has been attributed to about A.D. 1100. Beside the Fordwich Stone is the 'Penitent's Chair', found embedded in one of the church walls and also of great but unknown antiquity.

The river Stour at Fordwich is now a gentle and narrow waterway, and instead of seamen sailing in their ships to its harbour it is the boys of King's School, Canterbury, who are likely to be seen, drifting by, as they rest their oars on a summer's day.

14. Deal and Walmer

In the medieval period of power of the Cinque Ports, and in the 1668 Charter of Charles II, Deal and Walmer ranked as non-corporate members of Sandwich in the Cinque Ports pedigree; yet their importance became greater than that of their parent Head Port, for they remained coastal while Sandwich became marooned a couple of miles inland. From a defence point of view they occupied a vital stretch of shore, guarding the important Downs naval anchorage; and Walmer, since the early eighteenth century, has been especially honoured in providing the official residence of the Lord Warden of the Cinque Ports.

The castles at Deal and Walmer were part of a string of fortresses and blockhouses erected between 1539–40 for

82. Deal Castle, built by Henry VIII in 1539–40, remains a purely military fortress in character, its interior walls stern and bare and lacking the softening residential influence so noticeable at Walmer Castle.

defence of the coast against threatened invasion from the
Continent. The crisis arose owing to Henry VIII's defiance of
the Pope on the thorny problem of his divorce from Catherine
of Aragon and subsequent establishment of himself as head of
the Church of England. Excommunication followed in 1538,
and the Pope endeavoured with every means in his power to
enlist the might of François I of France and the Holy Roman
Emperor Charles V in a joint attack aimed at restoring England

83. Walmer Castle, built at the same time as Deal Castle and one mile distant, is
similar in design but totally different in aspect. Gardens and trees surround the
moat, structural alterations have taken place, and as the residence of the Lord
Warden of the Cinque Ports the Castle has inherited relics, memories, and a
general heritage of the great men who have resided there.

to the Papal fold. Charles V controlled the dangerously close
Netherlands ports. Had this invasion materialized one wonders
what the outcome would have been; but it never did—and
meantime Henry, with great speed, made preparations for
defence. The series of shore castles was constructed and these
bore no resemblance to any that had been built in this country
previously—for gunfire had become a new and dominant factor
in warfare.

Henry VIII's new castles took the form of a Tudor Rose, but there was nothing fanciful in this; the shape was designed to meet the new requirements of artillery. Unlike the mighty Norman and medieval keeps (which would have provided a target for naval gunfire) they were low and squat, with a series of semi-circular bastions each possessing tiers of guns; a gunport at the rear of the entrance hall provided for last-ditch defence.

The situation was indeed critical, for the King's army was much inferior to the combined forces of the French King and the Emperor and, with the power of the Cinque Ports in decline, his fleet was only in the early stages of its growth as a Royal Navy. Therefore, in the short time available for building adequate defences, Henry VIII concentrated on forts to protect the most vital anchorages. Ten of these castles were built, and only Sandown has failed to survive—for the small remnant of Sandown which can be seen at the northern end of the Deal shore can hardly be called a castle any longer. Sandgate Castle, near Folkestone, has also suffered such damage from the sea and the results of war that it is mainly the central tower that is left, giving it the appearance of a Martello Tower rather than one of Henry VIII's castles.

The rapid construction of Henry's fortifications was a remarkable feat, but it is intriguing to learn that this was not achieved without pay demands which threatened to hold up the whole operation. The records of building expenditure reveal that the labourers went on strike, demanding an increase from 5d. to 6d. per day—which only goes to show that times and people change less than one thinks.

The channel which stretches between this portion of the mainland and the treacherous Goodwin Sands is known as the Downs (and has nothing to do with the hills of Kent and Sussex of that name). In the days of sail this formed an excellent and much-used anchorage, usually sufficiently sheltered to accommodate large numbers of ships. To defend the Downs Henry VIII built three of his fortresses, the castles of Deal, Walmer and Sandown, each about one mile apart.

The castles never served the purpose for which they were built, and by the seventeenth century, when that indefatigable sightseer Celia Fiennes (granddaughter of Lord Saye and Sele of Broughton Castle, Oxfordshire) came to Deal, she seems to have been sadly unimpressed as far as the impregnability of the fortresses was concerned. She travelled on horseback, riding side-saddle, through the length and breadth of the land, and everything that she saw was of interest to her inquiring mind. Her pen was always ready to record all that caught her eye,

84. Lions of stone among the spring wallflowers at Walmer Castle. The gardens around the moat are usually ablaze with colour, and Dame Patti, wife of the present Lord Warden, Sir Robert Menzies, loves the flowers—as did the original creator of the Walmer Castle gardens, Lady Hester Stanhope, niece of William Pitt.

and it is the unaffected quality of her descriptions and comments that makes her *Journies* so appealing. Highwaymen, bad roads, lack of adequate maps—none of these handicaps deterred her. She summed up Henry's castles in a few scathing words:

'Thence we went to Deale 7 mile all by the sea side which is called the Downs, which sometymes is full of shipps all along the Road but now there were not many; the Downs seemes to be so open a place and the shoar so easye for landing I should think it no difficulty to land a good army of men in a little tyme, there is only 3 little forts or Castles they call them, about a miles distance one to another Warworth (Walmer) at Deal and Sandwich (Sandown?) which hold a few Guns but I think they would be of little effect and give the enemy no great trouble . . .'

Henry VIII would have turned in his grave to hear his fortresses dismissed so lightly, for we must credit him with having achieved a great deal in constructing so swiftly fortresses that were so solid, so totally different from any earlier strongholds in this country, and so well adapted to the new methods of warfare and defence.

A number of legends have been told regarding the unpredictable Goodwin Sands which lie roughly three miles to the east of Deal, between the North and South Forelands, and are still a danger to shipping. They have been the cause of a watery grave for many a ship and seaman, but when the winds are in the east or south-east they build up to form a breakwater and the sheltered anchorage of the Downs. When the tide ebbs and the sands dry out, they harden sufficiently to be walked upon (though no one is recommended to do so). Then, when the sea closes over the sands they become soft, shifting with the tide and building up unseen where previously ships could pass. Today three light vessels flash warnings to ships at sea, and there are also light buoys flashing their danger signals.

One of the stories told of the Goodwins is that in pre-Conquest days they formed a fertile island which was part of the vast territory owned by Earl Godwin, father of King Harold. Earl Godwin also held the Manor of Berkeley in Gloucestershire, and here, at Berkeley Castle, is still treasured today the superb Godwin Cup, from which he vowed to take Communion daily, whereupon no harm would come to his family or possessions; one day he failed in his vow—and the sea rose, engulfing his land on this part of the Kent shore and creating the ill-omened, wreck-strewn Goodwin Sands.

Another legend is that land now comprising the Goodwins was once protected by a stout sea wall. This fell into decay when stone allocated for its repair was used for the building of Tenterden's church steeple. A storm broke, the sea wall collapsed, and, so the story goes, the sea swept over the land creating the Goodwin Sands with their history of wrecks and tragedy. The combination of storms, wrecks and the shifting sands of the Goodwins certainly caused the blockage and silting up of Sandwich harbour, and frequent repetition of a local couplet has helped to lay the blame on Tenterden's shoulders. This runs:

> Of many people it hath been sayed
> That Tenterden steeple Sandwich haven hath decayed.

The story was embellished by the Protestant Bishop Latimer (1485–1555), who blamed an old Sandwich man approaching 100 years of age for the origin of the story. Latimer's version runs as follows:

'Maister More (Sir Thomas More) was once sent in commission into Kent, to help to trie out (if it might be) what was the cause of Goodwin Sandes and the shelfs that stopped up Sandwich Haven. Thether commeth Maister More, and calleth the countrye afore him, such as were thought to be men of experience, and men that could of likelihoode best certify him of that matter, concerning the stopping of the Sandwich Haven. Among others came in before him an olde man with a white head, and one that was thought to be a little less than an hundereth yeares old. When Maister More saw this aged man, he thought it expedient to heare him say his minde in this matter, for, being so olde a man, it was likely that he knew most of any man in that presence and company.

So Maister More called this olde aged man unto him, and sayd, "Father," sayd he, "tell me if ye can, what is the cause of this great arising of the sande and shelfs here about this haven, and which stop it up that no shippes can arrive here?"

"Forsooth, syr," quoth he, "I am an olde man: I thinke that Tenterton steeple is the cause of the Goodwin Sandes. For I am an olde man, syr," quoth he, "and I may remember

the building of Tenterton steeple, and I may remember
when there was no steeple at all there. And before that
Tenterton steeple was in building, there was no manner of
speaking of any flats or sands that stopped the haven; and
therefore I thinke that Tenterton steeple is the cause of the
destroying and decaying of Sandwich Haven.'''

On so slim a base does a legend spring to life. In Tenterden
it was long claimed that the story had its foundation in the
jealousy of neighbouring parishes because the beauty of Tenterden's new steeple surpassed their own; and when any
statement happened to prove wildly exaggerated, the people
of Tenterden would say that it was only as true as the story
of the Goodwin Sands and Tenterden steeple. But poor
Bishop Latimer, who regales us with the story of 'the old aged
man and Maister More', met his end by burning at the stake
during the reign of Mary Tudor.

Although the breakwater caused by favourable winds
created this sheltered anchorage of the Downs, there were also
times when violent storms blew up suddenly and the
ships in the Downs suffered severe losses. Such was the case
in November 1703 when one of the worst storms struck these
shores that has ever been recorded since the Great Storm of
1287. Damage was widespread, causing such terror that many
were convinced the Day of Judgment had come. Daniel
Defoe wrote 'Horror and confusion seized upon all; no pen
can describe it, no tongue can express it, no thought conceive
it, unless some of those who were in the extremity of it.' In
Kent alone, Defoe records, 1,107 dwellings and barns were
levelled. In the Downs this storm spelt disaster, and of the
ships of the fleet lying at anchor most were sunk, with the loss
of 1,500 officers and men.

Sudden storms proved beneficial to the British cause,
however, during the two landings of Julius Caesar along this
shore in 55 B.C. and 54 B.C. There has always been slight
contention about Julius Caesar's actual landing-place, but it
is most generally agreed that this was at Deal. Wherever
Julius Caesar and his men came ashore along this shifting
coast, however, it was certainly farther inland than the present

shoreline. Within days of his landing a storm broke of such ferocity that many of his vessels were destroyed, and Julius Caesar sailed away with his reduced and maimed fleet. The next year he returned, and again a storm broke, battering his ships unmercifully. It is not surprising that the later Claudian invasion of A.D. 43 took place at Sandwich (Richborough), where the then-existing channel of the Wantsum, between the Isle of Thanet and the mainland, provided more sheltered conditions.

Deal Castle has remained a fortress pure and simple through the centuries, almost unchanged today from the time when Henry VIII built it. For this reason the visitor senses very clearly, when exploring within its great bare walls, the atmosphere of national peril in which it was built.

Walmer Castle, on the other hand, has become much changed and softened in character by its use as the Lord Warden's residence, and to visit the two castles in turn is particularly interesting. Walmer has been added to structurally (though its Tudor design is still dominant), gardens bloom and mellow its whole aspect, and the Lords Warden who have lived here have left the mark of their individual personalities.

William Pitt brought with him to the Castle his headstrong niece, Lady Hester Stanhope, who acted as housekeeper, hostess and companion to her bachelor uncle both in London and at Walmer from 1803 until his death. She had a flair for landscape gardening, and her love of flowers and trees had its first creative outlet at Walmer, where her uncle's murmured wish for the softening effect of trees and foliage was enough to set her planning and planting. The yew hedges, flowers and trees that were to add so greatly to the beauty of the Walmer Castle scene were all laid out by Lady Hester Stanhope. A later Lord Warden, Lord Granville, interested himself greatly in the garden, but its birth was Lady Hester's achievement. Its beauty today would be the finest memorial she could have chosen, for her love of flowers was the gentlest side of this eccentric woman's character.

In 1810, life being altogether too tame for Lady Hester after her uncle's death, she left England for the Middle East, never to return. She lived the life of an Arabian queen on the slopes of Mount Lebanon, becoming an almost legendary figure. When she died in 1839 they buried her, with the English flag as her shroud, in the garden of her half-ruined Lebanese castle—a garden which she had created, transforming the dry barren soil into a fragrant oasis. She was not a person whom many people loved, but she was a sensational and unique personality.

There is a good deal of William Pitt's very fine furniture at Walmer Castle, and in his study is an interesting coloured print which portrays him as Colonel of the Cinque Ports Volunteers; also preserved here are the camp bed and folding chair which he used during his activities in this role.

But it is, in fact, the Duke of Wellington who steals the scene at Walmer Castle, and this is hardly surprising, for he lived here a great deal and, in the end, it was the place where he died. He was, also, the mightiest personality of the age. Wellington had a great affection for this austere home and, unlike William Pitt and Lady Hester, he had no wish to soften its austerity. A regime of military rigidity and simplicity was the order of the day during his occupancy, the only additional ornamentation in his time being the posting throughout the Castle of such stark notices as 'SHUT THIS DOOR'—unlikely to be misunderstood or disobeyed.

No one ever did disobey or attempt to deflect the Duke's spartan rules, and when Queen Victoria and the Prince Consort came to stay at the Castle in 1842 they were apparently delighted to find their visit accompanied by so little fuss. No fripperies at all were introduced to the rooms which they used, though the Duke did make one concession—the construction of a new window affording the Queen a spacious view of the sea which he felt she would enjoy should the weather be unsuitable for walking or sitting out of doors. The complete normality of everything so enchanted the Queen that she and the Prince Consort extended their stay—a breach of the pre-arranged schedule which is thought to have disturbed the Duke's orderly soul considerably. Every minute of his day and every day of his week must conform to premeditated plans, and it was surely a true test of his great devotion to the

Queen that he accepted this change of plan with such good grace.

The Duke of Wellington's bedroom-cum-sitting-room is approached by a staircase on which two portraits face each other, significantly from opposing walls—the Duke and the Emperor Napoleon. Then the spartan little room is reached in which the Duke lived and died. It is scarcely changed from his day, and a picture on the wall, which portrays the dying Wellington propped in the armchair in this room, depicts a scene in which almost every object remains in its same place today. The armchair stands unmoved from the centre of the room, its appearance faded but otherwise unchanged. Here is the Duke's tall writing-desk, for he preferred to work in a standing rather than sitting position. By the wall is the camp bed which accompanied him on his campaigns and which he would never exchange for anything more comfortable. On this bed his body was placed when he breathed his last on 14 September 1852.

The Duke had risen as usual the previous day, with no sign whatsoever of illness or weakness. No one in the land, least of all those close to him at Walmer, had any idea that his hours were numbered. He rode as was his custom and adhered to the routine of his day, retiring at the usual hour. The next morning at six-thirty a.m., his valet found him ill and moaning. His condition became increasingly worse as the day passed, and at four o'clock in the afternoon he died—in the old armchair which has never changed its position from that day to this. The shock to the world at large was doubly great because his end was so unheralded, and Longfellow wrote of his death:

> Meanwhile, without, the surly cannon waited,
> The sun rose bright o'erhead;
> Nothing in nature's aspect intimated
> That a great man was dead.

The dignity of the Duke of Wellington's lying-in-state and the fantastic pageantry of his funeral were far removed from the simplicity of the old soldier's way of life, and one cannot help feeling far closer to the true Wellington in his severe room at Walmer than in any other place where he is remembered. In

I

those first days after his death, however, everyone paid him homage with all the pomp and circumstance that his nature shunned—but how else could they do final honour to the victor of Waterloo?

A small museum of 'Wellingtonia' adjoins the Duke's bedroom, and here a particularly intriguing exhibit is the original pair of Wellington boots! Just as the fourth Earl of Sandwich will never be forgotten for inventing a quick and trouble-free snack, so the Duke of Wellington is remembered by all, even the most unmilitary and unhistorical, for his Wellington boots. For both young and old, it is a real event to see the originals in a glass case at Walmer Castle.

Other exhibits in this room include the last uniform coat worn by the Duke as Lord Warden of the Cinque Ports; his telescope and candle-lit lantern; his death mask. This mask is a sad relic which reveals a tired old man, an aspect by which we would most of us rather not remember a man so vital in his day. There are also a multitude of other relics and mementoes.

William Pitt and the Duke of Wellington have left memories which tend to overshadow those of other Lords Warden at Walmer, and one is conscious of a great feeling of regret at the Castle that one of the greatest Lords Warden of all, Sir Winston Churchill, never took up residence. His devotion to Chartwell was so deep that this was always his Kentish home, and all his relics and memories are concentrated there. The Lord Warden at the time of writing is the distinguished Australian statesman and former Prime Minister Sir Robert Menzies.

There is an interesting array of portraits of past Lords Warden at Walmer Castle, and also a list of the Constables of Dover Castle (the office combined from medieval times with that of Lord Warden). The Constables date from Earl Godwin in c. 1050 to Sir Robert Menzies today, and among the early Constables recorded are King Harold, Bishop Odo of Bayeux (half-brother of William the Conqueror), and Hubert de Burgh, victor of the famous sea battle which put an end to the attempt by Prince Louis of France to capture the English throne in 1216. The list was compiled by Brigadier Sir Hereward Wake, Bart., in 1931.

On leaving the Castle it is only a short walk to the earliest part of Walmer where the old church, which dates from Norman times, is hidden away in the thick foliage of the churchyard, and where the ruined walls of the eleventh-century moated manor house of the d'Auberville family stand with roofless dignity. The church is believed originally to have been the private chapel of this manor house. There are some charming Georgian buildings in this area, and in Walmer Castle Road another memory of the Duke of Wellington is encountered; here is the tall white Wellesley House whose plaque on the wall announces that 'Here lived Lieut. General Sir Arthur Wellesley, afterwards Duke of Wellington, before leaving for the Peninsular campaign in 1808'.

Deal has retained a much more bustling atmosphere than Walmer, an inheritance from the days when the town had an active Admiralty dockyard and was kept busy servicing the ships anchored in the Downs. This dockyard was demolished and used for building land in 1864, its site being immediately east of Deal Castle and north of the sea-front Prince of Wales Terrace.

The Time Ball Tower, which now houses Deal's Information Centre, was used as a semaphore tower for signalling messages from the Downs to London during the Napoleonic Wars. In 1855 it became the Time Ball Tower, and a copper time ball on a mast 14 feet high indicated the correct time to ships in the Downs. At 12.55 p.m. the ball was raised half-way up the mast, at 12.58 p.m. it reached the top, and at 1 p.m. it fell, released by electric current from Greenwich. In 1927 this custom came to an end, for time signals by radio made the service unnecessary.

Deal was granted a new coat of arms as recently as 1966. As the town is now a Corporate Member or 'limb' of Sandwich (instead of having only non-Corporate status as shown in the Charter of Charles II) the shield bears the three demi lions passant and three demi hulks of the Cinque Ports, also a wave surmounted by a silver oar. This oar, carried before the Mayor of Deal on ceremonial occasions, is a sign of sovereignty of the seas directly offshore, and the rank of admiral is automatically accorded to him when he visits Royal Navy

85. Middle Street, Deal. This picture shows Queen Anne House, with its neighbouring Dutch gable, many of which are still to be seen in the town and are, as in Sandwich, a heritage of the Protestant refugees from the Netherlands.

ships in local waters. The crest above the shield portrays the Tudor castles of Deal and Walmer.

There is great appeal in the old-world aspect of Deal, where small lanes or alleyways link the sea-front with the parallel Middle Street and High Street. Many eighteenth-century houses, large and small, have survived despite sad decimation of some areas during the Second World War, and what has survived of Middle Street, in particular, is a heritage to be cherished. Pride of place goes to the stately Queen Anne House, with the towering Dutch gable on the adjoining house (No. 11); such gables—quite plentiful in Deal when one looks around for them—are testimony of the architectural influence

86. Home of a famous 'Blue-stocking'. From 1762 to 1806 this house in Deal was the home of Mrs. Elizabeth Carter, scholar, translator of Epictetus, and friend of Dr. Johnson. The house is now an hotel.

of the Protestant refugees from the Netherlands who settled in the area.

Almost opposite Deal Castle an imposing range of buildings with a central cupola is the Royal Marines barracks and School of Music. The Royal Marines have been part of the life of the town ever since they first occupied the barracks over 100 years ago.

A dignified house in South Street, now the Carter House Hotel, was the home of Mrs. Elizabeth Carter. She was quite a notability in her day—a friend of Dr. Johnson, a scholar especially remembered for her translation of Epictetus, and a true 'blue-stocking'; yet she remained feminine, unaffected, and much loved by all. This house in Deal was her home from 1762 until her death in 1806, although she actually died in Clarges Street, London. Elizabeth Carter never married, but she always seems to have been known by the courtesy title of 'Mrs.'.

It is impossible to leave Deal and Walmer without a word or two on the third of this trio of Henry VIII's fortresses. What is left of Sandown Castle is to be found by exploring northwards along the front, but it is little more than a collection of stones which have been consolidated into some sort of shape in a too-late attempt at preservation. In the eighteenth century the sea battered it and encroached, then the Deal townspeople used its stones for building. There is, in fact, some wonder that the present small fragment survives. Only when gazing at this flimsy remnant of the third of Henry's Castles of the Downs does one tend to agree with Celia Fiennes that this 'would give the enemy no trouble'.

15. Dover

The tale of the Cinque Ports 'havens that hath decayed' is, at Dover, brought to an end—for Dover has not decayed but still stands on the seashore with a thriving harbour; it represents, as ever, 'the Gateway of England'. Like the rest of the Cinque Ports, Dover's history records plenty of harbour troubles, but they have been overcome; and with the cross-Channel ferries plying to and fro, the efficient car ferry terminal and the hovercraft service which carries passengers across the Channel so speedily, the Dover–Calais route remains the shortest and most popular sea crossing between England and the Continent.

In the past, owing to Dover's strategic position at the narrowest section of the Channel, it received greater royal support than any of the other Cinque Ports. During the reign of Henry III, for instance, Dover was given priority status for the entry of pilgrims and others to the country, and thereafter a flood of pilgrims to the shrine of St. Thomas Becket at Canterbury came and went via Dover's harbour. Later, when the harbour was endangered, the Tudors answered Dover's appeal for aid, when deaf ears were turned to requests from other Ports. Henry VIII listened to the problems of Sandwich and sympathized, but he did little. Queen Elizabeth's visits to Winchelsea and Sandwich in 1573 were the source of high hopes in these Ports, but material help for their declining fortunes did not result.

Dover's medieval harbour suffered severe damage when a massive cliff fall practically blocked it up, and it was with the support of the Tudor monarchs that the port was saved by rebuilding in the area of the present docks. In Henry VIII's time an embankment was constructed to form a protective barrier to the sea, and on this were erected a couple of towers intended to break the ferocity of the south-west winds and

87. King Charles II steps ashore at Dover on the Restoration of the Monarchy in 1660, as depicted in the well-known painting by Benjamin West.

also to provide mooring rings for vessels. These towers are seen prominently in the famous picture in the Queen's Collection which portrays the departure of Henry VIII in 1520 for the Field of the Cloth of Gold.

The sea was not to be deterred by these paltry measures. Only 10 years after Henry VIII's great assemblage of ships and nobility the embankment was so seriously damaged that the continued existence of the harbour was endangered, and one of the round towers which had seemed so sturdy had been completely washed away. But Queen Elizabeth proved an especially staunch friend to Dover, and with her support, followed by a long history of determination to outwit the elements, a fine harbour was constructed and has continued to grow and thrive up to the present day.

Through the centuries Dover has been the scene of many historic arrivals and departures. Here Richard I gathered together his knights and fleet before setting sail for the Holy Land and the Third Crusade. To Dover came Pandulf, the Pope's Legate, to receive King John's submission of the country to Papal control. From here, as already mentioned, sailed Henry VIII for the Field of the Cloth of Gold. And to Dover came Charles II on the Restoration of the Monarchy. Of these arrivals and departures, Pandulf's was the most humiliating, Henry VIII's the most spectacular, and Charles II's the most historic.

The purpose of Pandulf's journey makes melancholy reading. King John, having lost Normandy, had become embroiled in a feud with the Pope, Innocent III, over the nomination of the Archbishop of Canterbury. The quarrel between Church and Crown became as bitter and historic as that which had existed in his father's time and had resulted in the assassination of St. Thomas Becket. It ended in excommunication of the whole land, for under the Pope's interdict no priest could administer holy rites, the church bells were silent, the dead lay unburied—a terrible fate for any nation in medieval times, and a state of affairs which prevailed for many months. Finally the Pope issued a Bull of Deposition against the defiant King, a measure which John ignored as scornfully as the interdict.

Only when King John realized that enemies were combining on all sides to oppose him—the French, the Scots, the Welsh Princes, the English Barons—did he suddenly and unpredictably decide to outwit them all by surrendering England to the Papal See. And so, in May 1213, the Pope's Legate Pandulf landed at Dover, and the King, kneeling before him, spoke words unbelievable to English ears: 'I, John by the Grace of God, King of England and Lord of Ireland, for the expiation of my sins and of my own free will, and with the advice and consent of my Barons, do give unto the Church of Rome, and to Pope Innocent the Third, and to his successors, the Kingdoms of England and Ireland, together with all the rights

88. Dover Castle from the air. Behind the Norman keep (built by Henry II) can be seen the Church of St. Mary-in-Castro, with the Roman Pharos almost

touching it. In the centre foreground is St. John's Tower, and it is
beneath this area that the subterranean passages are located.

Aerofilms Ltd.

belonging to them, to hold them of the Pope as his vassal . . .'

After this it is less surprising that a group of rebellious Barons should have offered their support to the King of France with the object of placing his son, the Dauphin Louis, on the English throne. They believed that anything would be better than the continued rule of King John—and the wife of the Dauphin was the granddaughter of Henry II of England.

War resulted, during which Hubert de Burgh, Constable of Dover Castle, led the faction loyal to the King and withstood a stern siege of Dover Castle by the Dauphin Louis in 1216. That same year, however, both King John and Pope Innocent died. The child King Henry III ascended the throne, and Hubert de Burgh, with the men of the Cinque Ports, saved the country's independence by a great victory at sea which put an end to Prince Louis's aspirations.

Pandulf's arrival at Dover was an inglorious one, and it makes pleasanter reading to turn to the departure, in 1520, of Henry VIII for his meeting with François I of France at the Field of the Cloth of Gold. This is how the great occasion is described in the Dover Records: '. . . on the last day of May the King and the Queen, Thomas Wolsey, Cardinal of York, the Duke of Buckingham, Charles Duke of Suffolk, Maria Queen of France, wife of the Duke of Suffolk, the Archbishop of Canterbury, the Bishop of Durham, the Bishop of Ely, the Bishop of Chester, also the Earl of Northumberland, the Earl of Devon, the Earl of Shrewsbury, the Earl of Derby, the Earl of Worcester, the Earl of Wiltshire, the Earl of Westmoreland, the Earl of Kildare, and the Prior of St. John of Jerusalem in England, and very many other nobles, Knights and gentlemen, were carried across from Dover to the town of Calais at the charges of the Cinque Ports. (First the King and Queen and the rest as quickly as possible.) *But be it noted that never in the memory of man was seen so vast a multitude; so bravely arrayed and adorned—the servants as well as the nobles.*'

The return from exile of Charles II in May 1660 was a dramatic episode in Dover's history and, to quote again from the Dover Records, '. . . the King arrived in Dover Roads from Holland with twenty sail of His Majesty's great ships and frigates, the Right Hon. Edward Lord Montague being

89. Embarkation at Dover of Henry VIII for the Field of the Cloth of Gold, 1520. This picture, by an unknown artist, is in the Royal Collection.

General, and landed the same day.' The Records tell how General Monk first met the King upon a bridge 'let into the sea for His Majesty's more safe and convenient landing', and how, on the King coming from the bridge, he was met by the Mayor of Dover, who made a speech on his knees, and John Reading, Minister of the Gospel, who did likewise. The Dover Corporation presented him with a Bible, and it is related that 'His Gracious Majesty, laying his hand upon his breast, told Mr. Mayor nothing would be more dear to him than the Bible'. Quite a few things besides the Bible were going to prove very dear to Charles II in future years, but in that solemn moment he must have appeared most noble as he stood, hand on breast—an exile returned, and King of England on his native shore. Samuel Pepys described the reaction of the crowds at Dover, writing in his diary that 'the shouting and joy expressed by all is past imagination'.

In more recent times some notable arrivals of a different kind have been recorded. For instance, there was Louis Blériot of France who, in 1909, was the first man to fly the Channel. His memorial is the white outline of an aeroplane in a meadow close to the Castle, marking the place where his plane landed; in autumn and winter a good view of this is gained from the summit of the Castle Keep, but in summer the foliage of trees conceals it. Two memorials on the East Cliff Promenade are a reminder that the first man to make a return cross-Channel flight was the Hon. Charles S. Rolls in 1910, and that in 1875 Captain Matthew Webb was the first to swim the Channel.

But it is Dover's record in the last two World Wars that is as valiant as any time in the Port's history—the famous Dover Patrol of the First World War which guarded the Channel for Allied shipping and transports, and the stoicism of the citizens who endured the 'Hell Fire Corner' bombardment from 1940–44. Plans for the historic evacuation from Dunkirk were made in Dover Castle, an operation in which every small boat along these Cinque Port shores played its part in getting the men back to Britain.

The narrow Channel crossing has always dominated the life of Dover. On a clear day the cliffs of France are seen with startling clarity, and during the long years of the French Wars how uncomfortably close they must have seemed! To the people of France the White Cliffs of Dover doubtless aroused exactly similar emotions—emotions which are difficult to contemplate today. The French voices which are heard so frequently in the Castle and in the hotels of the sea-front seem part of Dover—and, in fact, are part of the Port's appeal; for Dover, although among the most British of all towns and ports, has also an international side to its character.

The relationship with France has always had curious side-lines in the whole area of the Cinque Ports, even in the worst centuries of war. The Huguenot refugees and their descendants had their links with France, and it was never possible to cancel out individual friendships and associations, even when war had been declared by higher authorities. And it must be remembered that, during the heyday of the old smuggling trade, this was not carried out on an insular basis. Vast numbers of the coastal families were involved, and the French seamen who met the smugglers in mid-Channel were their associates and friends. It was a natural friendship of close neighbours, far more intelligible today than the wars of the past, though these wars must figure in this book, for they dominated the lives of the people for many centuries.

There is something immensely likeable about the sea-front at Dover. One sighs for the gracious Regency crescent that was bombed out of existence during the Second World War, and I, for one, sigh even more deeply on looking at the straight line of the modern blocks of flats that have replaced it. But one impressive terrace of Regency architecture still remains as neighbour to the flats, and it seems a miracle that this has survived. One point on which the modern flats score, however, is in the flower beds which form their frontage—beautifully tended and bright with colour.

It is the lack of any form of commercialism on the sea-front that is so attractive at Dover, for most of its length is Harbour Board property. There are no shops, no ice-cream kiosks—just an atmosphere of peace in which to sit and watch the sailing-boats close at hand and the ships at sea, to enjoy the fresh salty air and listen to the cries of the gulls as they wheel overhead.

But it is always the Castle that dominates the Dover scene—from ships at sea, from the sea-front and from most parts of the town. Iron Age and Saxon earthworks were the first defence measures to occupy the Eastern Heights on which the Castle stands; then, with the arrival of the Romans, the Pharos was erected to guide the Roman ships into harbour. There was, in fact, a second Roman lighthouse on the Western Heights, but only traces of this remain.

The first Norman castle was a rapidly-built fortification which came into being almost immediately after the Battle of Hastings. This has disappeared altogether. The earliest parts

90. The Constable's Tower and Gate. This is the principal entrance to Dover Castle.

of the present Castle date from Henry II's reign, when the King expended massive sums of money on the construction of an impregnable stone fortress to replace the earlier stronghold. His work includes the massive Keep, and also the Inner Bailey's wall and towers. Additions were made by Richard I and King John, but it was Henry III who embarked on the most extensive building programme of all, completing the curtain walls and towers, building the great Constable's Tower which today provides the principal entrance to the

Castle, and making the fortress more suitable as a royal residence.

Henry III also constructed the circular St. John's Tower and spur of defences at the Castle's most vulnerable point—where the Dauphin Louis's siege operations had made apparent the need for stronger fortifications. Here underground tunnels linked St. John's Tower, the spur and the Castle. In the fifteenth century Edward IV built two more towers and made structural alterations to the Keep, while Henry VIII added, in the sixteenth century, what was known as the Tudor Bulwark to the south. The Napoleonic threat caused major alterations to the Castle, tower modifications being made to provide suitable gun emplacements. At this time additions were also made to the thirteenth-century underground passages.

Dover Castle has never been captured by any foe from outside these shores. Nevertheless, it *was* captured by a small group of Parliamentarians during the Civil War of the seventeenth century, when the Royalists had allowed the garrison to be reduced to a minimum. There was strong Cromwellian sympathy in Dover and, knowing the reduced state of the garrison, a local merchant named Drake and his fellow townsmen succeeded in breaking in, overpowering the guard, and seizing the Castle. Its unconquerable reputation was maintained thereafter, for the Royalists never succeeded in retaking it, and the Castle remained in Cromwellian hands for the duration of the Civil War. The mood had turned full circle by the end of the Cromwellian dictatorship, and the Royalist enthusiasm was overwhelming when Charles II stepped ashore at Dover in 1660.

The Statutes of Dover Castle are of great interest, for they were drawn up by Sir Stephen de Pencestre, Lord Warden of the Cinque Ports and Constable of the Castle, shortly after the Barons War ended with the victory of Henry III over Simon de Montfort at Evesham in 1265. These thirteenth-century Statutes mostly concern straightforward garrison rules and religious observances in the Church of St. Mary-in-Castro, but one or two are sufficiently intriguing to relate. For instance:

No. 4. It is established by ancient rule, that if a chief guard discovers a warder asleep, he shall take something from him as he lies, or carry away his staff, or cut a piece out of part of his clothes to witness against him in case the warder should deny having been asleep, and he shall lose his day's wage.

No. 6. Either sergeant or warder using vile language shall be brought before the Constable, who shall have the matter considered, and the offence fairly inquired into. He who was in the wrong shall lose his day's pay—if the Constable so wills.

No. 7. If a sergeant or warder strike another with the flat hand, he shall be liable to a fine as high as five shillings, and shall for the rest be held at the mercy of the Court. If he strikes with his fist he shall be liable to a fine as high as ten shillings and be at the mercy of the Court. If a sergeant or warder wound another the fine shall be as high as fifteen shillings, and the offender shall forfeit his station in the Castle, if the Constable so adjudge.

An additional Statute specifies that:

If the King arrives unexpectedly in the night, the gates shall not be opened to him, but he shall go to the postern called the King's Gate, towards the north and there the Constable and those who accompany him may admit the King and a certain number of his suite. When the King is admitted he has the command, and in the morning when it is full day, he may admit the remainder of his company.

This was obviously a safety measure to avoid opening the main gate after dark had fallen, but in winter the men must have spent an unenviable night on the exposed hilltop outside the walls.

Dover Castle served as a royal residence on many great occasions and especially for the reception of royal brides. Edward II brought here his bride, Isabella, later known as the 'she wolf of France'. They were a handsome pair then, and who could have suspected the future—that the King would die most horribly at the hands of a paid assassin in Berkeley Castle, and that his Queen would spend long years of imprisonment, on the command of her own son, as punishment for her evil deeds. Richard II met here his much-loved bride, Anne of Bohemia, and this was to prove a very different marriage from that of Edward II and Isabella. Charles I received here his bride, Henrietta Maria of France, whom he was to love dearly throughout their troubled life together; it is fortunate that she could have had no foreboding of the sad times ahead during that brilliant reception.

It seems remarkable that this great fortress has always escaped destruction. It was neglected after the Civil War, and at various times suffered injurious structural alterations; but the two perils which could have brought it to the ground passed it by. Its retention in Parliamentarian hands during the Civil War enabled it to escape the 'slighting' which, on Cromwell's orders, demolished so many of the Royalist strongholds; and somehow it was unharmed during Dover's long years of bombardment during the Second World War.

The visitor to Dover, however short his or her stay, should try not to miss a visit to the Castle. It is an outstanding example of a great military stronghold and is—as the official guidebook to the Castle points out—considered to be the earliest known example in this country and on the Continent of concentric fortification. In addition, its position on the summit of the Eastern Heights provides a magnificent viewpoint, especially from the top of the Keep. This, incidentally, is approached by a most reasonably wide newel staircase, so that those who dislike the perilously narrow and dark newel staircases usually found in medieval castles need not be deterred.

In the Keep itself there is a fine array of armour, a showcase displaying the robes of a Baron of the Cinque Ports worn at the Coronation of King Edward VII, and, for model battle enthusiasts, an enormous and enthralling model of the Battle of Waterloo. The beautiful little medieval Chapel of St. Thomas of Canterbury (within the Keep) is now used for prayer and occasional celebration of Holy Communion, but until its restoration in 1951 no service had been conducted in it since the Reformation.

The subterranean passages of the Castle hold constant and undiminished appeal for visitors, and especially for children. It is easy to distinguish the work of the different periods in these passages, for the great arched tunnels in the stone and chalk of the hillside are of the thirteenth century, and the brickwork passages are of the Napoleonic period. It has been suggested that the smaller crossway passage encountered at one point may have been made by the Dauphin Louis's men in their attempt to penetrate the Castle.

What appeals most of all to children in this subterranean network is the ingenious method of trapping prisoners. This belongs to the time of the Napoleonic threat, and the idea was that the enemy who succeeded in entering the Castle at this point would find that hidden doors had closed swiftly behind him, shut by a system of iron bars manipulated from the neighbouring guardroom. Once trapped, he (or they) would be at the mercy of the garrison. But these preparations were for the invasion which never came.

On entering this subterranean area today, the descent is first made by steps, followed by the steep and cavernous thirteenth-century tunnel which leads to a further descent in St. John's Tower. Then the route continues to the Napoleonic-period guardroom and the 'booby-trap' doors.

Apart from the imposing Constable's Tower exit, the gateway by which many visitors leave the Castle is in Peverell's Tower. This and several other towers in the curtain wall gained their names from the powerful Norman Barons who, in return for the lands they held, were responsible for the annual provision of an agreed number of knights and men-at-arms for the garrison. Peverell's Tower, incidentally, has a grim legend attached to it. When first under construction it kept collapsing and, to propitiate the evil spirits deemed to be at the root of the trouble, an old woman and her dog were buried alive in one of the walls—rather on the same principle as the fossilized cats found in the Stag Inn wall at Hastings. In this instance the old woman, before being encased, cursed the chief mason so heartily that when the building was completed he fell to his death from the top—a revenge which the poor Hastings cats were unable to put into operation.

Close to the Castle stands the Roman Pharos. Built early in the Roman Occupation, its exterior is octagonal and originally it rose to a height of 80 feet. There were eight storeys, then, but now only the first four storeys of the original Roman work remain. The Pharos was for centuries in a ruinous state owing to the reluctance of antiquaries to restore so historic a structure. In 1913, however, Earl Beauchamp (who later, as Lord Warden of the Cinque Ports, was responsible for the erection of the Shepway Cross at Hythe) embarked upon a limited and very successful restoration. The Pharos was not, in fact, over-restored; it was merely given a top storey and prevented from further deterioration.

Beside the Pharos is the ancient Church of St. Mary-in-Castro whose restoration, sad to say, cannot be claimed as an example of restraint. From pictures of this Saxon church before restoration in 1862 it is clear that it had fallen into a ruinous state, but the Victorian mosaics which disfigure almost the whole of its walls were surely unnecessary. Sir George Gilbert Scott restored the church, but the mosaics were added 20 years later so he cannot be blamed for them. When St. Mary's was built the Saxons used a great deal of material from existing Roman buildings, and Roman bricks are still visible in large numbers; more would certainly be visible if the unsightly mosaics could be removed.

On recovering from the shock of the mural ornamentation of St. Mary-in-Castro, it is realized what a marvellous church this would be could it be de-restored. A Saxon doorway (bricked up but splendid) survives in the south wall, and there is a gracefully-vaulted chancel with rounded chancel arch of massive solidity; there are deeply splayed windows and much else of interest to discover. For instance, a fine example of a child's coffin stone is attributed to the Saxon period, and several examples of Roman floor tiling are preserved (one with the imprint of an animal's foot in it!). At the northern base of the chancel arch is a stone with three circles, a symbol of the Holy Trinity believed to have been scratched by one of the many Canterbury pilgrims of medieval times who passed this way. A showcase contains a small collection of Roman and other 'finds' in the vicinity—among which I noticed part of a human jaw with so fine a trio of teeth that they put present-day decayed and mended versions to shame; there must be something seriously wrong with our diet that we cannot reach the grave with as good teeth as these. The date of the jaw was not given.

At the west end of the church is the only surviving bell, dated 1639, but this was one of comparatively late date for a record exists of bell repairs in the years 1286–7. In the four-teenth century two new bells were cast and hung in the Pharos which, being adjacent to St. Mary-in-Castro, was used as a belfry. In the eighteenth century these bells mysteriously disappeared, and only the 1639 one remains. St. Mary-in-Castro has served as both a parish and garrison church, and at the time that Sir Stephen de Pencestre compiled his Statutes of the Castle it is clear that there was a separate soldiers' altar.

From the Roman Pharos and the Roman bricks of the Saxon church, it is logical for one's thoughts to turn to the Roman Fort of the Saxon Shore at Dover. Of these nine forts, five were on the Cinque Ports coast and the location of only one had, until recently, eluded discovery. This was at Dover. Now it has been found. In July 1970 clearance work started in the Queen Street area in preparation for the construction of a new road, and the fort was discovered, together with the earlier Roman Classis Britannica Fort. Teams of volunteers have been digging on the two sites during 1970 and 1971, and during the 1970 operation alone up to 20,000 finds were made, including tiles stamped with the initials CLBR, representing the Classis Britannica, the fleet of Roman Britain.

The South and West walls of the Saxon Shore Fort have been revealed, together with two bastions and the defensive ditch, and from the excavations to date it is considered that the fort dates from the third century A.D. The Classis Britannica Fort, which the Saxon Shore Fort is considered to have super-seded, is thought to be of the second century A.D. It was on the site of this earlier fort that a specially treasured find came to light—a small bronze of a hand holding an orb with an Imperial Eagle perched upon it. These excavations have gone a long way towards proving that Dover was the headquarters of the Roman fleet in Britain. (This is the latest information to date, from Brian Philp's Interim Report in the Kent Archaeological Review.)

Turning again to Norman Dover, the Maison Dieu (which now forms part of the Town Hall buildings) was founded by Hubert de Burgh in 1203 for the purpose of offering free overnight lodging to the pilgrims arriving from the Continent on their way to Canterbury. Later, wounded and sick soldiers returning from the wars were accommodated there, and eventually a few permanent pensioners were accepted; thus, by degrees, the character of the Maison Dieu changed from a pilgrims' hostel to a pensioners' hospital.

Henry VIII brought the Maison Dieu, as such, to an end in 1544, and after being put to various uses the surviving building, in a serious state of disrepair, was acquired by the Dover Corporation in 1834. It was restored by Ambrose Poynter and William Burges, and the latter's well-known enthusiasm for the neo-baronial style of architecture is immediately apparent. The result has concealed the old building, but nevertheless it presents a fine hall of great dignity.

The Maison Dieu has a special significance in any account of the Cinque Ports Confederation. Its founder, Hubert de Burgh, was Lord Warden of the Cinque Ports; on the walls hang portraits of a number of distinguished Lords Warden of the past; from the upper walls hang the old colours of the Cinque Ports Volunteers, raised in the times of emergency of 1794 and 1803; and most fascinating of all is the original banner of the Cinque Ports which was used each year at the opening of the Yarmouth Herring Fair. Now framed and carefully preserved, this banner occupies the wall behind the mayoral chair in the council chamber. Among the paintings in the council chamber is a portrait of Queen Elizabeth I, by an unknown artist but of special interest as a contemporary portrait; the Dover Corporation purchased it in 1598 for 25 shillings. In the background of the portrait is a series of small figures representing the virtues.

In Priory Road, only a very short distance from the Maison Dieu, is the tiny and beautifully-restored thirteenth-century Chapel of St. Edmund. This is of outstanding interest. Having

91. **The Chapel of St. Edmund,** Dover. This thirteenth-century chapel, dedicated to St. Edmund of Abingdon, was consecrated by St. Richard of Chichester on 30 March 1253, a few days before his death in the nearby Maison Dieu.

become very derelict it was, in 1965, threatened with demolition, and has been saved only by determination of a truly dedicated kind. In its restoration only materials of the medieval period have been used.

To have lost the little chapel would have been a disaster. It was founded to serve the Cemetery of the Poor and has a claim to uniqueness—that it is the only standing chapel consecrated by an English canonized saint in honour of another

English canonized saint. Dedicated to St. Edmund of Abingdon, Archbishop of Canterbury, it was consecrated by St.
Richard of Chichester, who knew, loved and venerated St.
Edmund. On 30 March 1253, St. Richard stood in the chapel
and expressed his joy in performing the consecration. His
words, converted into modern English, were, '. . . it has
been my deepest wish—something I have prayed for with all
my strength—that before my death I should consecrate at
least one church to his memory. From the very depths of my
heart I thank God that He has not cheated me of my heart's
desire. And now, brethren, I know that I am shortly to die and
I commend my soul to your prayers.'

So St. Richard left the Chapel of St. Edmund, walked the
short distance back to the Maison Dieu where he was staying,
and only four days later, in the Maison Dieu, he died. For long
afterwards the chapel fulfilled its role in the Cemetery of the
Poor, and it also became a place to which pilgrims made their
way. Then, in 1544, like so many religious foundations in
Henry VIII's time, the Maison Dieu was forced to offer its
submission to the Crown—and St. Edmund's Chapel was
included with it.

As time went by the tiny chapel, whose consecration had
brought such pleasure to St. Richard's last days, literally
disappeared from sight, for buildings enclosed it on all sides;
but worse was in store with the threat of demolition. The
Chapel of St. Edmund was saved, however, and in May,
1968, it was reconsecrated. It stands, quietly and unobtrusively,
only a short distance from the Maison Dieu and the busy
traffic of Biggin Street; it can easily be missed—but most
certainly should not be.

Dover College is a very short walk from the chapel, and
this well-known boys' school occupies the land and surviving
buildings of the twelfth-century Priory of St. Martin. The
remains of the great Priory Church were demolished in the
mid-nineteenth century, but several of the fine conventual
buildings have been ably restored and are used by the school.

Anyone approaching Dover College via the entry from
Effingham Crescent will find that there is, on one of the gateposts, a helpful map showing the layout of the old and new

92. The Priory Close at Dover College where the Installation meeting of the Court of Shepway is held. Dover College occupies the land and surviving buildings of the twelfth-century Priory of St. Martin. The old Priory Gatehouse (now the school library) is seen in this picture.

buildings. To the left, across the Close (and near to the Priory Road railway station entrance) will be seen the old Priory Gatehouse, a most picturesque building which now serves as the School Library. On the opposite side of the Close is the Priory Guest House, a fine twelfth-century survival which is now the school chapel. Closer to Effingham Crescent is the Priory Refectory, now the school hall and used for functions and the performance of plays. This is a magnificent hall, and in it are the remains of a twelfth-century wall painting which stretched the whole width of one end of the hall; if this could have been saved what a treasure it would have been. The painting portrayed the Last Supper, but during Victorian

Kent Messenger.

93. Sir Robert Menzies arrives at the Maison Dieu at Dover on the occasion of his installation as Lord Warden of the Cinque Ports in 1966. Sir Robert is glancing upwards, his attention caught by a foliage kangaroo among the decorations.

attempts at restoration it was irreparably damaged, and later efforts to remedy the Victorian work only made matters worse. Today little can be seen other than traces of the halo marks, the gilding of which had made indentations in the wall.

Dover has, of course, always played an important role in the affairs of the Confederation of the Cinque Ports, the Lord Warden of the Cinque Ports and the Constable of the Castle being a joint appointment. The installation of a new Lord Warden is a great day of ceremony and celebration, for, this being a life appointment, it is not a frequent occurrence. The various installation events are divided between the Castle, the Priory Close at Dover College, and the Maison Dieu.

On Installation Day all the dignitaries gather at Dover Castle, where the new Lord Warden inspects a guard of honour, a band plays, and he is ceremonially handed the key of the Castle by the Deputy Constable. The installation service is then held in the Church of St. Mary-in-Castro, and the installation proceedings of the Court of Shepway take place in a marquee erected in the Priory Close of Dover College. A banquet in the Connaught Hall of the Maison Dieu completes the day's celebrations.

Throughout the day the Sergeant of Admiralty carries the Silver Oar in front of the Lord Warden—the symbol of authority of the Cinque Ports, which serves the same purpose as a mace. In 1966 (at the installation of the present Lord Warden, Sir Robert Menzies) the historic seventeenth-century oar was carried; since then it has been lost through a burglary at the Dover Museum and at the time of writing has not been recovered. A replica has replaced it, but the theft of the seventeenth-century oar is a sad loss.

The installation of Sir Robert Menzies was a memorable day for Dover and the Cinque Ports, and everyone was hoping that fine weather would accompany the great occasion. But the day before the installation was one of pouring rain and high winds, and hopes began to fade. That evening the Archbishop of Canterbury, Dr. Ramsey (who was to conduct the installation service in the Church of St. Mary-in-Castro), dined in the Constable's Tower with the Deputy Constable; and as they listened to the howling of the wind, and the beating of rain as it swept against the massive tower, the prospects of a fine-weather installation seemed dim. When they parted for the night, the Archbishop said, 'I shall pray for a fine day tomorrow'. His prayers were answered, for the next morning everyone awoke to brilliant sunshine and clear skies, and the sun shone throughout the whole day's celebrations. Since then, the unfailing annual visit of Sir Robert and Dame Patti from Australia to the Lord Warden's residence at Walmer Castle has been a feature of the year for the Cinque Ports.

Although St. Mary-in-Castro on Castle Hill is where the installation service is held, the Church of St. Mary-the-Virgin in Cannon Street is the parish church of Dover, and its sturdy Norman tower is a splendid sight. The rest of the church has suffered greatly from nineteenth-century restoration and rebuilding, and during the Second World War the windows were blown out and the clock and bells damaged. It seems miraculous that St. Mary's survived at all, for two shells fell in the churchyard and 30 more within a radius of 200 yards; but the great tower survives, and is the architectural treasure of this part of the town. In the south-west corner of the church is the Bench of the Barons of the Cinque Ports, in the centre of which is the raised seat of the Lord Warden. This bench was originally in the ancient Church of St. James at Dover, but on its destruction during the Second World War the bench was retrieved, restored, and placed in St. Mary's. In past days the Chancery Court of the Confederation of the Cinque Ports used to be held in St. James's Church.

Dover's Museum (in the Town Hall buildings) contains a fascinating mixture of items of local, general, or antiquarian interest, all gathered together in a very limited space. Here, for instance, can be seen the 'Dover Treasure Trove' of 685 ancient coins found in the neighbourhood of Market Street. The hoard contained two groats of Edward I's reign, and of these the museum holds only copies, for the originals are in the British Museum. The rest of the coins are the originals. It has been suggested that the whole hoard was buried hastily in 1295 when the French fleet was sighted, and it was in the subsequent landing of French forces that Dover was sacked and burnt.

Among the Cinque Ports exhibits in the museum is a beautifully compiled Chronicle (hand-written and illustrated) of the Wardens of the Ports and the Constables of Dover Castle.

The Roman items now number far too many for exhibition in the small space available, for many thousands of pieces of Roman date have emerged from the excavations in the York Street and Queen Street areas. The exhibits range from treasures to curiosities, from stuffed animals to Roman glass, from Wedgwood china to a collection of coats-of-arms spoons. When I was there in March 1971 the museum had just, during the previous week, received a collection of 9,000 birds' eggs, said to be one of the best collections in Europe.

For children—and, of course, for adults too—there are a number of tableaux in the museum depicting Bronze Age Dover, Iron Age Dover, Roman Dubris, Dover in the Dark Ages. The scene is always the same, with the figures of the period standing on the clifftop—and beside each tableau is an informative note, together with a small collection of finds of the period concerned.

Dover is the one Head Port of the Confederation that remains an important port to this day, and it is appropriate that its Corporate Members, Folkestone, Margate and Faversham, should still be thriving places too. Folkestone, now a large town, combines the role of cross-Channel port and resort most successfully. Faversham is an ancient town whose maritime privileges, granted in the time of Edward the Confessor, were confirmed by Royal Charter in 1252. Here King Stephen (who reigned from 1135–54), his Queen Matilda and son Eustace, were all buried in the great royal abbey which has proved, since excavation of the site in 1965, to have been larger than Westminster Abbey in Edward the Confessor's day or Canterbury as built by Lanfranc.

Dover, the Cinque Port which has never lost its maritime status, completes this tour of the Cinque Ports and Romney Marsh. All that is left is to tell the tale of the century of storms, culminating in the Great Storm of 1287. This was the most momentous period in the annals of the Confederation—and the forerunner of its decline.

16. Century of Storms and the Great Storm of 1287

The series of storms for which the thirteenth century was remarkable is recorded in lurid style by the chroniclers and historians of former times. These accounts make enthralling and appropriate reading, for the impact of this tempestuous century struck so devastatingly at the Cinque Ports that as a whole the Confederation never recovered its former prosperity and dominance. It is easy to grasp, as one reads these descriptions, the sense of powerlessness against the elements which must have overcome these medieval people. They were a tough, seafaring race, but here was an enemy against whom no amount of courage or strategy could bring victory.

In the 1230's the sea began to creep mercilessly towards Old Winchelsea. In 1241, although it was not a year of storms, the weather caused widespread hardship throughout the whole land, and the phenomenon of the excessive heat of summer and cold of winter is recorded by Matthew Paris in the following words:

'This year was on the whole tolerably abundant in crops of fruit and corn; but from the feast of the Annunciation of the Blessed Virgin till that of the apostles Simon and Jude a continued drought and intolerable heat dried up deep lakes and extensive marshes, drained many rivers, parched up the warrens and suspended the working of mills; hence the pastures withered away, herbage died, and consequently the flocks and herds pined away with hunger and thirst. In the winter, too, namely about the Advent of our Lord, ice and snow, attended by intolerably severe cold, covered the earth, and hardened it to such a degree, at the same time freezing the rivers, that such great numbers of birds died, that the like was never remembered to have occurred before.'

This was only a preliminary to the evils to come. In 1250 a storm broke which is recorded by Holinshed:

'On the first day of October the moon, upon her change appearing exceeding red and swelled, began to show tokens of the great tempest of wind that followed, which was so huge and mightie, both by land and sea, that the like had not been lightlie knowne, and seldome, or rather never heard of by men alive. The sea, forced contrarie to his natural course, flowed twice without ebbing, yielding such a rooring that the same was heard, not without great woonder, a farre distance from the shore. Moreover, the same sea appeared in the darke of the night to burn, as it had been on fire, and the waves to strive and fight togither after a marvellous sort, so that the mariners could not devise how to save their ships where they laie at anchor, by no cunning or shift that they could devise. At Hert-burne three tall ships perished without recoverie, besides other smaller vessels. At Winchelsey, besides other hurte that was done, in bridges, milles, breakes, and banks, there were 300 houses and some churches drowned with the high rising of the watercourse.'

Only two years later, in 1252, another massive storm broke which is recorded by Matthew Paris:

'On the octave of Epiphany, in the year 1252, during the day and night a terrible south-west wind prevailed. It drove the ships from their anchorage, raised the roofs of houses, many of which were thrown down, uprooted completely the largest trees, deprived churches of their spires, made the lead to move, and did other great damage by land, and still greater by sea, and especially at the port of Winchelsea, which is of such use to England and above all to the inhabitants of London. The waves of the sea broke its banks, swelling the neighbouring rivers, knocked down the mills and the houses, and carried away a number of drowned men. And at the close of the following year the sea again broke its bounds, and left so much salt upon the land that in the autumn of 1254 the wheat and other crops could not be gathered as usual and even the forest trees and hedges could not put out their full foliage.'

Then came the catastrophic storm of 1287, which finished Old Winchelsea and crippled Romney so disastrously—the tempest of which Camden wrote, in 1586, 'What time the face of the earth both here, and also in the coast of Kent neere bordering, became much-changed.' So the Century of Storms came to an end, and with these vivid early descriptions, which I know I cannot better, the time has come to end this book, too.

Bibliography

General

A Calendar of the White and Black Books of the Cinque Ports, edited by
Dr. Felix Hull, Kent County Archivist (1966).
The Constitutional History of the Cinque Ports by K. M. E. Murray
(1935).
Charters of the Cinque Ports by Samuel Jeake (1728).
History and Topographical Survey of the County of Kent by E. Hasted
(1797–1801).
Kent History Illustrated by Frank W. Jessup (1966).
The Cinque Ports by Ronald and Frank Jessup (1952).
The Heraldry of the Cinque Ports by Geoffrey Williams (1971).
Kent and the Cinque Ports (pictorial) by H. R. Pratt Boorman (1957).
The Coastline of England (geological) by J. A. Steers (1948) and *The
Sea Coast* (1962).
Victoria County History.

Romney Marsh

The Level and the Liberty of Romney Marsh by M. Teichman Derville
(1936).
The History of Romney Marsh by William Holloway (1849).
Romney Marsh by Walter J. C. Murray (1953).
Romney Marsh by John Piper (1950).

Histories of Individual Ports

The Records of Dover by John Bavington Jones (1920).
History of the Town and Port of Dover and Dover Castle by the Rev.
John Lyon (1813).
Historic Haven (Sandwich) by Dorothy Gardiner.
The History of Antiquities of the Ancient Town and Port of Rye by
William Holloway (1847).
A New History of Rye by Leopold Amon Vidler (1934).
The History of Winchelsea by William Durrant Cooper (1850).

Local Publications

A Guide to Romney Marsh by Anne Roper, and her individual guides
to a number of churches of the Marsh.

Discovering Deal by Barbara Collins (Deal Borough Council, 1969).
The Ancient Town of Hythe and St. Leonard's Church by the Rev.
Herbert D. Dale.
St. Edmund's Chapel, Dover, and its Restoration, by Terence Edmund
Tanner.
Borough of Hastings publications by W. H. Dyer.
The Story of Lamb House, Rye by H. Montgomery Hyde (1966).

Hastings Museum Publications
The Cinque Ports and Coronation Services by J. Manwaring Baines.
Outline of Hastings History by J. Manwaring Baines.

Rye Museum Publications
William Holloway, Historian of Rye by Geoffrey S. Bagley.
Old inns and ale-houses of Rye by Geoffrey S. Bagley
Many a Bloody Affray (Rye Smugglers) by Kenneth M. Clark.

H.M. Stationery Office Publications
The Roman Forts of the Saxon Shore by Leonard Cottrell.
Guide to Dover Castle by R. Allen Brown
Guide to Richborough Castle by J. P. Bushe-Fox.
Deal and Walmer Castles by A. D. Saunders.

Index